A Study on the Book of James

Rev. David D. Wilson

PARADISE GOSPEL PRESS

A STUDY ON THE BOOK OF JAMES, Wilson, David D.

First Edition

PARADISE GOSPEL PRESS
www.paradisegospelpress.com

Song Lyrics in the Public Domain:

To Be Like Jesus
The Old-Fashioned Meeting
Abide With Me

ISBN: 978-1-946823-05-2

Table of Contents

James

Acknowledgment

Bibliography

Answers

Introduction

There is conflict about James and who he really was. Some believe he was **James the Elder, the brother of John, the son of Zebedee**. Others believe he was **James the Less, the son of Alphaeus**. Yet another group believes he was **James the Just, the brother of our Lord and Saviour Jesus Christ**. To be truthful, it makes no difference as to his pedigree or genealogy. We know that James, the brother of Jesus, lived in Jerusalem.

Paul records in Galatians that he went to Jerusalem to see Peter and stayed with him for fifteen days. **While there, he saw James, the brother of our Lord.**

Galatians 1:18-20

18 Then after three years I went up to Jerusalem to see Peter, and abode with him fifteen days.
19 But other of the apostles saw I none, save James the Lord's brother.
20 Now the things which I write unto you, behold, before God, I lie not.

It is a common belief that James was not a believer in

Jesus being the promised redeemer until after His death and resurrection from the dead. Paul states that Jesus was seen of about five hundred souls at one time, and afterwards, He went and showed Himself to James, His brother.

1 Corinthians 15:6-8

> *6 After that, he was seen of above five hundred brethren at once; of whom the greater part remain unto this present, but some are fallen asleep.*
> *7 After that, he was seen of James; then of all the apostles.*
> *8 And last of all he was seen of me also, as of one born out of due time.*

Whereupon **James believed that Jesus was the Lord and Saviour**, just as He had said. After seeing Jesus, James **devoted his life to the service of our Lord**. He grew in the service of the Lord to the point that he became the **head of the Jerusalem Christian church**. His life was a witness and an example of righteousness and holiness before God. It is reported that James continually **gave himself to prayer before God** for the people, that God would forgive their sins and save them.

As we know from the Word, James, although a Christian, was still **very closely tied to the Jewish law** and customs. Paul at one time had to persuade James that the Gentiles could be saved and their sins forgiven through Jesus' blood; and that the **Gentiles did not and in fact could not live for God if they had to abide by Jewish law** and dietary customs, which were in direct opposition to the Gentile way of life.

After this meeting, the Gentile church grew and spread rapidly. The thing Paul stressed to James was that the **Gentiles'** salvation was based upon living for God according to the teachings of the gospel and not Jewish traditions. Even though James relented to Paul on the matter of the Gentile Christians, he did not intend to give up his Jewish ways of living. Paul was as much a Jew as James and far more educated in the Jewish laws and customs; the difference was Paul's calling to the Gentiles.

James was called to the Jewish Christians in and around Jerusalem. From papers written about James by the early church fathers, we can tell a lot about James. James was tied to the legalism of the Jewish faith, yet at the same time, he was a practical and moral man. James loved the church, and his love of the Christian church led to his death. He was killed by the Jews, beaten to death at the age of ninety-five.

Chapter 1

James 1:1

James, a servant of God and of the Lord Jesus Christ, to the twelve tribes which are scattered abroad, greeting.

James begins by telling us who he is, **a servant (a slave) to God and to the Lord Jesus Christ**. This James is a far cry from the man he was when Jesus was alive. As far as anyone knows, Jesus was not accepted by His brothers and sisters as the promised Messiah. Jesus made the statement that a prophet is without honor in His own house.

Matthew 13:57

And they were offended in him. But Jesus said unto them, A prophet is not without honour, save in his own country, and in his own house.

Mark 6:4

But Jesus said unto them, A prophet is not without honour, but in his own country, and among his own kin, and in his own house.

John 7:5

For neither did his brethren believe in him.

In the home where Jesus grew up, we see Joseph, Mary, Jesus, James, Joses, Judas, Simon, and some sisters who are not named. What a family it must have been! The Messiah, rejected by His own brothers and sisters. James was tied to the Jewish faith and customs. **Even as head of the church in Jerusalem, he still held to the legalistic traditions and dietary customs of the Jews.** What caused James to become a Christian? When Jesus died upon the cross and was placed into the tomb, He rose from the dead, alive again. Jesus then appeared to the twelve, and He was seen of some five hundred at one time. After these appearances, Jesus made a special appearance, and that was **to His brother, James**. From that day forward, James **believed in Jesus as God's only Son**, the Redeemer of mankind.

1 Corinthians 15:5-7

[5] And that he was seen of Cephas, then of the twelve:
[6] After that, he was seen of above five hundred brethren at once; of whom the greater part remain unto this present, but some are fallen asleep.
[7] After that, he was seen of James; then of all the apostles.

If you wonder why I am going over what I covered in the introduction, we sometimes miss vital information. This is too important to let slip away. As we continued into verse thirteen, we find Jesus' mother, Mary, James and the rest of Jesus' brothers **assembled in the upper room** with the disciples and others.

Acts 1:13-14

> *13 And when they were come in, they went up into an upper room, where abode both Peter, and James, and John, and Andrew, Philip, and Thomas, Bartholomew, and Matthew, James the son of Alphaeus, and Simon Zelotes, and Judas the brother of James.*
> *14 These all continued with one accord in prayer and supplication, with the women, and Mary the mother of Jesus, and with his brethren.*

Jesus appearing to James caused a **complete turnaround in James' life**. It is also believed that **James is responsible for his brothers coming to accept Jesus** as the Lord of their lives. Little is known of their lives except for Judas, better known as Jude. This same Jude is the Jude who wrote the New Testament book of Jude.

We know because as Jude introduces himself, he gives claim to being the brother of James. We can see by looking at James how **one person obeying the gospel can and does make a world of difference** in the service of the Lord and in this evil world in which we live.

As we look at the times in which James lived (and eventually became head of the Jerusalem church), we see that in the church's infancy, most of the Christians were Jews. **James, being a Jew, knew the laws of legalistic Judaism,** even the dietary ones. This put James **in the right place at the right time**.

The church was in a time of transition. The Christian church was **breaking free of Judaism with its legalistic way of life**. As we see James, we know that he did not intend to leave his Jewish upbringing; and even as head of the church he was still very legalistic. We know that **Paul had to persuade James that the Gentiles could be saved** through the blood of Jesus. Paul also had to persuade the council in Jerusalem as well as James that these Gentiles could live for God by simply **living according to the teaching of the gospel**. The Gentiles could not serve God if all the legalistic Jewish traditions and the Law of Moses bound them. Their whole lifestyle, **their way of living was as different from the Jews as night and day**. Paul's work was toward the Gentiles while James stayed with the Jerusalem church until his death.

The death of James is not recorded in the Bible. However, we do find **a record of his death in *The Complete Works of Josephus***. Here we find that at the death of Festus, the high priest Ananus took upon himself to call a council of the Sanhedrin. He had James brought before it, **accused James of breaking the law and condemned him to death**. The high priest had James stoned. It is said that James was thrown from the gable of the temple and finally beaten to death with a club. Listed below is Josephus's account of what happened to James.

The Complete Works of Josephus tells us:

> And now Caesar, upon hearing the death of Festus, sent Albinus into Judea, as procurator. But the king deprived Joseph of the high priesthood, and bestowed the succession to that dignity on the son of Ananus, who was also himself called

14

Ananus. Now the report goes that this eldest Ananus proved a most fortunate man; for he had five sons who had all performed the office of a high priest to God, and who had himself enjoyed that dignity a long time formerly, which had never happened to any other of our high priests. But this younger Ananus, who, as we have told you already, took the high priesthood, was a bold man in his temper, and very insolent; he was also of the sect of the Sadducees, who are very rigid in judging offenders, above all the rest of the Jews, as we have already observed; when, therefore, Ananus was of this disposition, he thought he had now a proper opportunity [to exercise his authority]. Festus was now dead, and Albinus was but upon the road; so he assembled the sanhedrim of judges, and brought before them the brother of Jesus, who was called Christ, whose name was James, and some others, [or, some of his companions]; and when he had formed an accusation against them as breakers of the law, he delivered them to be stoned: but as for those who seemed the most equitable of the citizens, and such as were the most uneasy at the breach of the laws, they disliked what was done; they also sent to the king [Agrippa], desiring him to send to Ananus that he should act so no more, for that what he had already done was not to be justified;

Tradition says that James prayed for those who were casting stones at him, where upon one of them took a fuller's club and beat James in the head till he died.

The book of James was written **to the members of the twelve tribes**, which were scattered abroad. The people James wrote to were Christians, **both Jews and Gentiles**, who lived out-side of Israel. Remember on the day of Pentecost when Peter preached to the multitude. There were Jews there from different parts of the known world. **Peter called these people brethren, as does James in his epistle**.

Each time God brought judgement upon Israel, He **scattered the people into foreign lands**. There were Jewish com-munities in most of the large cities in the surrounding countries and throughout the then-known world. There were Jews in Alexandria, Egypt, and all the way up to Rome. There were Jews in Cappadocia, Pontus, Pamphylia, Antioch, Corinth, Philippi, Ephesus, Derbe and many more cities—even Babylon.

In the early days of the fledging church, **most Christians were Jews**, but not all, for God was **beginning to bring the Gentiles into the church**. The Jews on the other hand were rejecting the Gentile Christians because they did not abide by the Law of Moses or live by the Jewish customs and traditions. Just as today, there were divisions in the church. Some demanded that **everyone had to live by Jewish customs and law**. Others were leaving the Jewish religion and trying to live by the teachings of the gospel. There was **confusion in the church**, and some who were not qualified wanted to become leaders and teachers in the church.

The problem was **spiritual immaturity in the church**. To gain respect we must be what we profess to be. Our lives must show that we are **mature enough to handle ourselves wisely**, knowing what must be done. Therein lies the problem of the local churches. Not many were mature enough (or grounded enough) in the gospel message to lead the flock of God. There was a big difference between **wanting to be a leader or teacher and being mature enough in wisdom and judgement to be that leader**.

We know that **whom the Lord calls, He also qualifies**. There were times in my first pastorate that I questioned if God knew what He was doing when He called me to pastor a church. I had to trust him and spend time on my knees and in the Word. Today we continue to deal with spiritual immaturity in the church. Too often we associate maturity with age, and in the natural world this is usually the case. Yet, in the spiritual, **this rule does not necessarily apply**. Spiritual growth varies with each individual. A person can be older in years and be spiritually very immature; or younger in years but very mature in the spiritual realm with God. **Spiritual growth has nothing to do with natural age**. There must be a **continual growing of the spiritual man or we fail God**.

The Wiersbe Bible Commentary: NT states:

> Spiritual maturity is one of the greatest needs in churches today. Too many churches are playpens for babies instead of workshops for adults. The members are not mature enough to eat the solid spiritual food that they need, so they have to be fed on milk (Heb.5:11-14). Just look at the problems James dealt with and you can see that each of them is characteristic of little children:
> Impatience in difficulties – 1:1-4
> Talking but not living the truth – 2:14ff
> No control of the tongue – 3:1ff
> Fighting and coveting – 4:1ff
> Collecting material "toys" – 5:1ff

The purpose of the church is to reach the lost for Christ. To complete the task that is set before us, we must **first learn some very important lessons**.

We must learn how to **get along together without infighting** among ourselves. The battle, the fight, is not inside the church (or it should not be). The battle is outside of the church in the world where sin has complete control over hearts and lives. We must learn that to be a good leader, we must first learn **how to be a good follower**. One example is to look at Joshua. He was a great leader, but to get to that place he had to **follow Moses for over forty years**. The disciples became the great apostles, but to reach their calling they had to **sit and learn at Jesus' feet for three and one-half years**. We cannot become spiritual giants overnight.

Even Paul had to get away and be taught of the Lord. After Paul's sight was restored, he preached Christ to the Jews in Damascus where he was rejected of them. Paul declares that he **left Damascus and went into Arabia for three years**.

Galatians 1:17-18

> [17] *Neither went I up to Jerusalem to them which were apostles before me; but I went into Arabia, and returned again unto Damascus.*
> [18] *Then after three years I went up to Jerusalem to see Peter, and abode with him fifteen days.*

What Paul did in Arabia we can only guess. However, it stands to reason that the time was spent in prayer and study; and that he was under instruction by the Lord as to what he was to preach and teach and to whom he was to carry the Lord's message of the gospel. **We must learn patience with people if we are to reach them for Christ.** We must always **show forth the love of Christ.** Always tell the truth to those we meet. **Never lie to people.** Never be two-faced. **Always be what we profess to be.**

James' desire was to help the Jews that were scattered over the known world. As Peter preached on the day of Pentecost, thousands were saved. As they left Jerusalem and went back to their homes, they **took the message of Christ with them**, where they started local assemblies or churches.

It is to these Christians that James is writing. He desires to help them solve some of their problems in their service of the Lord. **Remember that to be a good teacher, we must first be a good student.**

James 1:2

My brethren, count it all joy when ye fall into divers temptations;

James begins by addressing the saints as brethren. This included both Jews and Gentiles. **The nationality or origin of a person makes no difference to the Lord.** The Lord looks at the **soul of a person, not the land** of their birth. Before Jesus came and began to establish the New Testament or New Covenant with man, God looked at national Israel as His sole people. The only hope the outsider or Gentile had was to be proselyted into the Jewish faith.

After the birth of Jesus, when He began His ministry, Jesus did not **look at a man or woman's nationality but at their soul**, at their faith. We are all the sheep of God's pastures. We are **all called of God to salvation, to whosoever will.** The decision is ours to make. As the body of Christ, as the church, we are brothers and sisters in Christ. **We are a spiritual family.**

James goes on to encourage the church, the body of believers, by telling them to **"count it all joy"** when they fall into temptations. Temptations do a work within us for our good. As crazy as it sounds, **temptations will build our spiritual faith in God**. We need a spiritual boost from time to time. Every battle that we fight and win **encourages us to trust in Jesus more and more**. Each victory helps us to **stand on our faith in God**.

The trials of life push us out of our comfort zone. Just like the eagle has to stir up her nest to make the young eagles leave it, so must God **stir up our lives to cause us to step out in faith**, to trust and believe. In this life, we will go through many kinds of trials and tests. We must remember that **we are not alone**. The Lord walks close by our sides. Tests are designed by the Lord to **build us up in different areas of our spiritual lives**.

You may ask in what areas. Some tests are to mature us, to instill wisdom and knowledge in us that **we may be a help to those who are around us**. It is hard to help someone going through a trial or test **if we have not been through it ourselves**. We read in verse four of this chapter:

James 1:4

But let patience have her perfect work, that ye may be perfect and entire, wanting nothing.

To be of any use to the Lord, we must, let me repeat it again, we **must become spiritually mature**. We must let every test, trial, and temptation **become a steppingstone on our journey to perfection** in Christ Jesus. The saved, born-again

20

Christian is called by the spirit of God to become a member of God's holy family. As part of this family, it becomes our job, our goal to **reach the lost with the gospel**. We cannot make people accept the Lord; all we can do is to **give them the opportunity**. It becomes their responsibility before God what they choose to do with the gospel message.

As Christians, we are to remember that **we are a part of God's scattered people, not God's sheltered people**. Each trial and temptation is for our benefit to make us stronger in the Lord. As long as we walk close to God and trust in Him, we can **overcome everything this world can throw at us**. We can have peace and joy in the face of trials because Jesus is with us. Always remember that **you are not alone**. For *"greater is He that is in you, than he that is in the world."*

James 1:3-4

³ Knowing this, that the trying of your faith worketh patience.
⁴ But let patience have her perfect work, that ye may be perfect and entire, wanting nothing.

As Christians, our lives are going to be watched by the world. You may think that nobody is watching and that nobody is listening to what you are saying. However, I can assure you that you are very much mistaken. People are judging your life every day. They **watch you to see how you handle yourself in the everyday trials** and troubles that come your way.

Too many times I have seen how people judge others. I worked with a man some years ago who claimed to be a good Christian. He talked much about going to church and told people

21

how good he was. Then one day, some things happened at work that concerned him. He got extremely mad and used ungodly language. He carried on and on about the situation. While this was taking place, I had different ones come to me and say, "I thought he was a Christian." All I could do was to say, "Well, he claims to be a Christian." Their answers to me were, "Well, he does not act like it," and there was not much I could say.

Our lives should be lived as if they are an open book without anything to hide. We need to live the way Jesus lived, to be open before others. We know the world is going to condemn us. We do not need to give them any ammunition to use against us. We are going to face enough trials without us causing more.

There are several different reasons why our faith is tried and tested. **When our faith is put to the test, it is for our own good, our benefit.** I know it is hard to see any good in trials and temptations, but I can assure you that God knows what He is doing. Trust Him.

One reason is that the trying of your faith teaches you patience. The only way to gain patience is by **going through trials and temptations**. So, if you are praying for God to give you more patience, then **be prepared for trials and temptations** to come your way.

Multiplied trials and tests are hard as we go through them. However, with every victory, our faith and patience grows. This learning process is sometimes grievous, but although we weep in the night, **victory and joy comes in the morning**. Patience is learning to wait upon the Lord.

Isaiah 40:31

But they that wait upon the LORD shall renew their

strength; they shall mount up with wings as eagles; they shall run, and not be weary; and they shall walk, and not faint.

There is an old saying and I find it to be very true. It goes like this: "God is never early, but He is never late. He is always just in time." I do not know who first said these words, but they are oh, so true. **God always comes through just in time.**

I remember part of the words to a song about Lazarus being dead. When Jesus came to the tomb of Lazarus, he had been dead four days, the chorus to the song says, ". . . four days late but just in time." The Lord will **always come to your aid just in time**. Never fear, only believe.

To live this Christian life we **must learn to have patience**. We must learn to wait. Never, ever think that we can fix our problems and trials; be assured that trying to fix them ourselves is a certain way to make them worse. **To win the victory we must "Trust and obey for there is no other way."**

A second way that trials are good for us is because they **help mature us spiritually**. If you are unstable in your Christian life, you are not dependable to God. God is seeking men and women who will be willing to **stand in the gap and make up the hedge** regardless of the cost we must pay.

Our faith in God is the most important part of our Christian walk. We read in I Peter where Peter wrote, "Beloved, think it not strange concerning the fiery trial which is to try you."

1 Peter 4:12-13

[12] Beloved, think it not strange concerning the fiery trial which is to try you, as though some strange thing

happened unto you:

¹³ But rejoice, inasmuch as ye are partakers of Christ's sufferings; that, when his glory shall be revealed, ye may be glad also with exceeding joy.

Brothers and sisters, **trials are a part of the believer's life**. They mold and make us into what God desires for us to be. A mature Christian is an **asset to God and His work** here on earth. Immature Christians are impatient and rush ahead without using wisdom and understanding.

Wisdom, knowledge, and understanding are distinguishing traits of a mature child of God. They come by going through the trials of life. We can read all the books written on how to live an overcoming life, how to gain patience, how to have faith, but as good as some of them may be, **the only way to have patience and build faith is by going through trials** and temptations.

While I am talking about books, I recommend that you read books by Smith Wigglesworth such as *Ever Increasing Faith* and *On the Power of Scripture*. I have found Wigglesworth's writings very inspirational in my life. Always remember that God will **not put more on us than we are able** to bear. In addition, with every temptation, **God will make a way to escape**.

1 Corinthians 10:13

There hath no temptation taken you but such as is common to man: but God is faithful, who will not suffer you to be tempted above that ye are able; but will with the temptation also make a way to escape, that ye may be able to bear it.

24

The Wiersbe Bible Commentary: NT tells us:

> The only way the Lord can develop patience and character in our lives is through trials. Endurance cannot be attained by reading a book (even this one), listening to a sermon, or even praying a prayer. We must go through the difficulties of life, trust God, and obey Him. The result will be patience and character. Knowing this, we can face trials joyfully. We know what trials will do in us and for us, and we know that the end result will bring glory to God.
>
> This fact explains why studying the Bible helps us grow in patience (Rom. 15:4). As we read about Abraham, Joseph, Moses, David, and even our Lord, we realize that God has a purpose in trials. God fulfills His purpose as we trust Him. There is no substitute for an understanding mind. Satan can defeat the ignorant believer, but he cannot overcome the Christian who knows his Bible and understands the purposes of God.

In verse four, James begins by saying to *"let patience have her perfect work."* What is he really saying? He is saying that **through patience we become perfect** in the sight of Almighty God. Here we see that it is God's desire that we be perfect before Him. Yes, I know some people say that no one can be perfect. However, I believe what the Bible says when it tells us to be perfect. What is perfect?

Webster's New World College Dictionary gives this definition:

> In a condition of complete excellence, as in skill or quantity; faultless; most excellent, sometimes used comparatively; "to create a more perfect union"

I believe that God intends for us to **live a perfect life in His sight**. We do this by living an overcoming life before God. The problem most people have is that they do not know the difference between temptation and sin. I know that I repeat this over and over; however, you need to get it settled in your mind. It is not a sin to be tempted; sin only comes in **when we yield to the temptation**. Most people believe that when they are tempted, they have already sinned, and this is not true. **Sin only comes when we do what the devil has tempted us to do.**

Now as for being perfect in the sight of God, I can name at least four men in the Bible, besides Jesus, that were perfect. **Adam and Eve were perfect before they fell** to the devil's lies and sinned. We find also in Genesis that **Noah was perfect in his generation**. In the book of Job, scripture states that **Job was a perfect and upright man** in the sight of the Lord. Enoch and Elijah were perfect because **God took them into heaven without having died**. The scriptures tell us that no sin can enter into heaven, so it must make sense that they had to be perfect in God's sight. **Just as these men were perfect, before God, we are expected to be perfect, also.**

The scripture ends with this, *"that ye may be perfect and entire wanting nothing."* Wanting nothing implies being complete or fully developed, not immature and not a novice. We also find Jesus telling us to be perfect. Therefore, if no one can be perfect as many proclaim, why does our Lord tell us to be perfect?

Matthew 5:48

> *Be ye therefore perfect, even as your Father which is in heaven is perfect.*

Paul, as with James, weighs in and tells the Christians **to be perfect in the sight of the Lord**.

2 Corinthians 13:11

> *Finally, brethren, farewell. Be perfect, be of good comfort, be of one mind, live in peace; and the God of love and peace shall be with you.*

Why do people, teachers and even ministers try to explain away the scriptures?

James also speaks of patience, meaning to wait calmly. You will find many things in this life that demand patience or waiting. Raised on a farm, when our crops were planted, all we could do was wait upon God to give the harvest. **Patience is a virtue that every Christian should have** and must have to please God. So, as we face trials and temptations, we are to do it **joyfully and with patience**, knowing that our Heavenly Father loves us, is **perfecting us and getting us ready to join Him** in heaven.

Praise God, the rapture is soon to take place. Jesus is coming after His Bride and we are going home to the place that has been prepared for us. As the Word says, where Jesus is, there we shall be also, forever with the Lord.

James 1:5-8

⁵ *If any of you lack wisdom, let him ask of God, that giveth to all men liberally, and upbraideth not; and it shall be given him.*
⁶ *But let him ask in faith, nothing wavering. For he that wavereth is like a wave of the sea driven with the wind and tossed.*
⁷ *For let not that man think that he shall receive any thing of the Lord.*
⁸ *A double minded man is unstable in all his ways.*

In these four verses there is one main thought presented. But we need to take a close look at these verses individually, because in them, there is a **wealth of information that we need to glean**. Too many times, we seem to overlook important facts that can help us in understanding the full meaning of God's Word. This fifth verse is such a verse. It begins: *"If any of you lack wisdom."*

We must first ask, "What is wisdom?"

The answer can be confusing. We often think of wisdom and knowledge as being the same thing; however, I can assure you otherwise. Knowledge is the ability to **take something apart**, and wisdom is the ability to **put it back together**. This may seem funny, but all too often this is the case. It does not take wisdom to take something apart, because anyone can do that. Wisdom, however, is **figuring out how to reassemble it** so that it works.

Knowledge is learning about all manner of things. There are books full of knowledge. I had a cousin who read the encyclopedia at home; he enjoyed learning about the world and the things in it. As far as book learning, he was very knowledgeable. I have seen and known men with degrees hanging on their walls, smart men, their hearts full of knowledge. Yet, they had no idea how to put what they knew into practical application.

Wisdom is practical application, knowing how to take your knowledge and make it work for you. I worked with an engineer once who could draw up plans on paper, and when we took those plans, we could build it perfectly. However, although he could draw it, he could not build what he had drawn. **Wisdom is far more than the intelligent acquisition of knowledge; it is putting into practice what we have learned.**

James is giving the saints of his day and the saints of today some very important advice. If you lack wisdom, then go before God and **ask for the wisdom that comes from above**. God's wisdom helps as we go through the trials of life. A man or woman of God will **use this wisdom to take the opportunity to learn** from every trial they face. James tells us that if we will ask God for wisdom, God will give it to us liberally. What does the scripture say? *"Seek and ye shall find, knock and it shall be opened unto you, ask and it shall be given unto you."* To go along with this, the scriptures also teach that *"ye have not because ye ask not."*

Matthew 7:7-8

> *[7] Ask, and it shall be given you; seek, and ye shall find; knock, and it shall be opened unto you:*
> *[8] For every one that asketh receiveth; and he that seeketh findeth; and to him that knocketh it shall be opened.*

James 4:2

> *Ye lust, and have not: ye kill, and desire to have, and*

cannot obtain: ye fight and war, yet ye have not, because ye ask not.

Matthew 21:22

And all things, whatsoever ye shall ask in prayer, believing, ye shall receive.

To receive, we must **believe what the Word teaches**. Without believing there will be no receiving.

James 1:6

But let him ask in faith, nothing wavering. For he that wavereth is like a wave of the sea driven with the wind and tossed.

In verse six, James reminds us that we must have faith, nothing wavering. In other words, **we must believe**. Believing in God and His Word is having faith. Many times, we tell people to **only believe and God will meet their needs**. In truth, what we are saying is to **have faith and God will make a way**. James goes on to say that if we waiver, we are untrustworthy. We are like the waves of the sea, driven about by the winds; a wishy-washy person is of no use to God.

Webster's New World College Dictionary says wishy-washy is:

1. watery; insipid
2. a: weak, feeble
   b: vacillating; indecisive

A wavering Christian is all of the above. One minute they are up, and the next minute they are down. Sadly, the churches are full of this type of Christian. There can be several reasons why we find a person in this state; however, the main one to me is indecision. All sorts of people fall into this class; not willing to make a decision because it might be the wrong one, they are constantly changing their minds. In Revelation 21 we find a list that tells us who will not be in heaven. At the head of this list is the fearful and next the unbelieving.

Revelation 21:8

> *But the fearful, and unbelieving, and the abominable, and murderers, and whoremongers, and sorcerers, and idolaters, and all liars, shall have their part in the lake which burneth with fire and brimstone: which is the second death.*

To overcome this condition, it is **so important that a Christian gets rooted and grounded in God's Word**. Why? Because God's Word is forever established; it never wavers.

Ephesians 4:14

> *That we henceforth be no more children, tossed to and fro, and carried about with every wind of doctrine, by the sleight of men, and cunning craftiness, whereby they lie in wait to deceive;*

We must have faith, because **faith makes all the difference in the hearts and lives** of men and women. In Hebrews 11:1

31

we read: *"Now faith is the substance of things hoped for, the evidence of things not seen,"*

Barnes' Notes on the New Testament tells us:

> We cannot hope to obtain any favour from God if there is not faith; and where, as in regard to the *wisdom* necessary to guide us, we are sure that it is in accordance with his will to grant it to us, we may come to him with the utmost confidence, the most entire assurance, that it will be granted. In this case, we should come to God without a doubt that, if we ask with a proper spirit, the very thing that we ask will be bestowed on us.

Faith is an unquestioning belief in God and His Holy Word, a belief when everything tells you that there is no use, and yet **you believe anyway knowing that God has heard your prayer**, your petition. Let us look at what the dictionary gives as the definition of faith.

Webster's New World College Dictionary defines faith as:

1. unquestioning belief that does not require proof or evidence
2. unquestioning belief in God, religious tenets, ect.
3. complete trust, confidence, or reliance

I know the world does not and cannot understand the true Christian, the real child of God, the born-again believer. It is their loss and the Christian's gain to have someone like Jesus who will

32

never leave us nor forsake us. He is **with us when everything is falling apart**. He gives us **peace in the best and in the worst** of times. We can always depend on Jesus, our Saviour and big brother. Along with Jesus we have a Heavenly Father who **loves us and cares for us**. It cannot get any better than this.

Remember, when you pray, **pray with faith, believing and with nothing wavering**. We all must admit that at times we find ourselves in the same place as the father who brought his son to the disciples to be healed of a dumb spirit. They prayed for the boy; however, he was still possessed. Then Jesus came upon the scene and asked what was going on. The father of the child told Jesus that his son was possessed of a dumb spirit from childhood, that he had come to get his son delivered of the demon spirit. The disciples could not cast out the demon spirit.

Jesus told the boy's father to **only believe, for all things are possible to him that believeth**. Here is where we find ourselves many times. We are in prayer, and with tears, we pray, *"Lord I believe; help thou mine unbelief."* **Jesus honored the father's truthfulness; his son was set free.**

Mark 9:19-27

> *[19] He answereth him, and saith, O faithless generation, how long shall I be with you? how long shall I suffer you? bring him unto me.*
> *[20] And they brought him unto him: and when he saw him, straightway the spirit tare him; and he fell on the ground, and wallowed foaming.*
> *[21] And he asked his father, How long is it ago since this came unto him? And he said, Of a child.*
> *[22] And ofttimes it hath cast him into the fire, and into the*

waters, to destroy him: but if thou canst do any thing, have compassion on us, and help us.

²³ Jesus said unto him, If thou canst believe, all things are possible to him that believeth.

²⁴ And straightway the father of the child cried out, and said with tears, Lord, I believe; help thou mine unbelief.

²⁵ When Jesus saw that the people came running together, he rebuked the foul spirit, saying unto him, Thou dumb and deaf spirit, I charge thee, come out of him, and enter no more into him.

²⁶ And the spirit cried, and rent him sore, and came out of him: and he was as one dead; insomuch that many said, He is dead.

²⁷ But Jesus took him by the hand, and lifted him up; and he arose.

We must never forget that Jesus loves us. He loves us so much that He was **willing to die upon the cross for us**. He knows that at times we may be pushed to our limits, but He will **always make a way for us**. We may have to search for it, but never fear, it is there. There are times I have had to pray, *"Lord I believe, help my unbelief,"* and Jesus has never failed me. He will **never fail you, either**. Just believe in Him and see the hand of the Lord at work. Have faith, for **in Christ Jesus all things are possible**. Do not let the devil cause you to be found wavering.

James 1:7

For let not that man think that he shall receive any thing of the Lord.

In verse seven, the scripture is very plain. The man or

woman that wavers or is indecisive need not think that they will receive anything from the Lord. Just as in the past, the fearfulness that rules so many hearts today puts up a wall between man and God. This wall shows God that the indecisive Christian is not dependable and is not established upon the solid rock, the Word of God. The scripture expressly states that *"having done all, to stand."* **That's God's requirement of us, to simply stand on His Word.**

Ephesians 6:13-14

> [13] *Wherefore take unto you the whole armour of God, that ye may be able to withstand in the evil day, and having done all, to stand.*
> [14] *Stand therefore, having your loins girt about with truth, and having on the breastplate of righteousness;*

Christians must learn to **stand for our Lord and Saviour.** One of the most important things we can do in our walk with the Lord is learn *how* to stand. This is so vital that I have listed **eight additional scriptures for instruction on how to stand for God.**

Romans 14:4

> *Who art thou that judgest another man's servant? to his own master he standeth or falleth. Yea, he shall be holden up: for God is able to make him stand.*

1 Corinthians 16:13

> *Watch ye, stand fast in the faith, quit you like men, be strong.*

Galatians 5:1

Stand fast therefore in the liberty wherewith Christ hath made us free, and be not entangled again with the yoke of bondage.

Philippians 1:27

Only let your conversation be as it becometh the gospel of Christ: that whether I come and see you, or else be absent, I may hear of your affairs, that ye stand fast in one spirit, with one mind striving together for the faith of the gospel;

Philippians 4:1

Therefore, my brethren dearly beloved and longed for, my joy and crown, so stand fast in the Lord, my dearly beloved.

1 Thessalonians 3:8

For now we live, if ye stand fast in the Lord.

2 Thessalonians 2:2, 15

That ye be not soon shaken in mind, or be troubled, neither by spirit, nor by word, nor by letter as from us, as that the day of Christ is at hand. Therefore, brethren, stand fast, and hold the traditions which ye have been taught, whether by word, or our epistle.

1 Peter 5:12

By Silvanus, a faithful brother unto you, as I suppose, I have written briefly, exhorting, and testifying that this is the true grace of God wherein ye stand.

If we are to receive anything from the Lord, we must show Him that we are **willing to stand**; that regardless of the cost, **we will stand**. I have seen Christians pray that God would save their children, their sons and/or daughters **regardless of the cost, whatever God had to do** to get them saved. Then something happens to their lost loved ones. They get hurt or terribly sick, and they run to God for their healing or for whatever they need to fix their problem. I believe that many times we truly do not know what we are praying for when we pray, "Save them, no matter the cost." Many have had to **reach death's door before God could get their attention**.

There are many who think that I am wrong; however, I would rather see a person **receive Jesus as their Saviour on their deathbed and go on to heaven** than to be healed, only to go back into the world at the mercy of Satan. I would rather **know that they were in heaven, where I will be with them again**, than for them to be lost forever. To receive anything from our Lord, we must stand fast upon the Word. To waver is to receive nothing but heartache and pain.

James 1:8

A double minded man is unstable in all his ways.

In verse eight, James clears everything up by saying that a double-minded man is unstable in all his ways. When we second-guess everything, we are showing immaturity, that we are unable to make up our minds. There will be times in this life when we will make wrong decisions, and we must learn from them. **Admit when you make a mistake, go on, and serve the Lord.** We must learn to trust in our Lord. This walk with God is a partnership. This is a **trust relationship between the Lord and his people**.

As we read God's Word, we must learn the lessons the Lord has put there for us. Abraham **trusted God, even when God told him to offer up Isaac**, his son, as a burnt offering. As Abraham trusted in God and prepared to offer up Isaac, God **provided Abraham with a lamb to take Isaac's place**.

Joseph **trusted God while he worked in servitude**. He trusted God while he was **in prison and God gave him the victory**. **God used Joseph to save Joseph's family** from starvation.

Moses trusted in the Lord and God gave **deliverance to the Israelites**. Moses led the people in obedience to God's plan. Moses should be an example to us, to ask God's will in our lives, and then **obey the voice of God**. Moses led the people, the Israelites, to the Red Sea. Pharaoh and his army were in pursuit. The people were afraid because there was nowhere for them to go.

They cried out to Moses who went and cried out to the Lord. After Moses talked to the Lord, the Lord gave Moses instructions. Moses went before the people and said unto them, *"Fear ye not, stand still, and see the salvation of the Lord, which he will shew to you today: for the Egyptians whom ye have seen today, ye shall see them again no more for ever."* (Exodus 14:13) Moses **listened to the voice of the Lord and obeyed**. Only one time did Moses disobey, and because Moses acted in himself, not under the direction of God, he was not allowed to go into the

Promised Land. **When we obey the Lord, God gives us the victory.**

David, against the giant Goliath, went forth **in the name of the Lord and God gave the victory**. You may say, "But David won the victory." However, it was God who **guided that stone to the right place to kill Goliath**. We, like Abraham, Moses, David and all the rest of God's heroes, must be **of a single mind, a mind that is stayed** on the Lord.

The double-minded person cannot make up their mind; they are indecisive in all their ways. Do you go right, left, or maybe straight ahead? Do you walk in faith or unbelief? Are you a real Christian or a counterfeit Christian? All these questions we must answer for ourselves, for we are the only one besides God who knows the answer. If you are immature or unstable, you will find that you will face times of fear and even torment. Trials cause the immature Christian to grow and mature, whereas the unstable person, the person who wavers, will find no peace until they learn to stand upon the Word of God. We must become focused upon *"thus sayeth the Lord."* We must become **single minded when it comes to God and His Word**. We must accept the fact that God is "My God." No matter what the world around us has to say, we must **accept the fact that He is "My God."** Then and only then will we receive the peace that comes from God.

James 1:9

Let the brother of low degree rejoice in that he is exalted:

In verse nine we find a truth that is often pasted over. *"Let the brother of low degree rejoice."* Of low degree could mean a poor person or a person who is not held in high esteem in the community. Whatever the cause of his low degree (or ours) it makes no difference to our Lord. Jesus says unto all, "Come unto me," and **He will not cast us out**. When we meet Jesus and repent, we are **adopted into the family of God**.

Our spiritual status goes from low to high in the matter of a heartbeat. We become **kings and priests unto God**. We go from a spiritual pauper to king's kids in the time it takes to pray and repent. Our souls are lifted up, and **there is a joy and peace that we have never known**. We may be poor in this world, but we are rich in spirit. Our heavenly Father **meets all our needs according to His riches in glory**. The scriptures tell us that God owns all the cattle on a thousand hills, and He makes us glad. Rejoice in the Lord for He is God. He is the **friend who comes to us in the middle of the night** to dispel all our fears.

James 1:11-12

[11] For the sun is no sooner risen with a burning heat, but it withereth the grass, and the flower thereof falleth, and the grace of the fashion of it perisheth: so also shall the rich man fade away in his ways.
[12] Blessed is the man that endureth temptation: for when he is tried, he shall receive the crown of life, which the Lord hath promised to them that love him.

In the churches of today as in the churches of James' day, the same problems rise to the surface. One of the main problems has to do with social status. In many churches there are some who are well off financially. Then there are those who are poor. Though this should not be a problem, it too often is. At times, people who have money think they deserve more privileges than poor folks. This thought also carries over to the people who give a lot of money to the church.

People who are what we call "high donors" can falter from God's path and begin to think they deserve the right to run the affairs of the church. When they do not get their way, they pout and withhold their finances. When this occurs, the only thing that the church can do is **go to the Lord in prayer**. God is **good at leveling the field** by putting trials and tests in the offender's life. Even the rich, the well off, when sincere before God, **repent and accept God's will for their lives**. Our God knows how to lift up the poor and to bring low the rich of this world. Let's look at a quote from the Rev. John Phillips on James.

The John Phillips Commentary Series tells us:

> There is nothing particularly spiritual about being poor, and there is nothing particularly sinful about being rich. Temptations exist at both extremes. In His parable of the sower (Matt. 13), the Lord Jesus pointed to the thorns that choked out part of the harvest. He said that the thorns represented "the care of this world," the great problem of the poor, and "the deceitfulness of riches," the great problem of the rich (v. 13). Worry on the one hand and wealth on the other, both of which "choke the word" (v. 22). The wise man prayed, "Give me neither poverty nor riches; feed me with food convenient for me: lest I be full, and deny thee, and say, Who is the LORD? or lest I be poor, and steal, and take the name of my God in vain" (Prov. 30:8-9).

James used an illustration that everyone could understand, an example from nature. He speaks of how the hot sun withers the grass and burns it with heat until it fades away; and so it is also with the rich. They shall fade away and all that they have will do them no good. The lesson that mankind needs to learn is that **this life will soon be past and only what we do for Christ will last**. As it has been said, it is not a sin to be rich. It is, however, a sin to trust in the riches of this world and not to trust in the Lord.

In the Old Testament, the more prosperous a person was in the goods of this world, the more he was blessed of the Lord. However, in the New Testament, Jesus began to teach that **it was a sin to trust in riches**. That the man who trusted in riches would never get into heaven. We must remember the words of Jesus as He talked to the man who asked what he had to do to enter into the glorious kingdom of God and have eternal life.

Mark 10:17-22

> [17] *And when he was gone forth into the way, there came one running, and kneeled to him, and asked him, Good Master, what shall I do that I may inherit eternal life?*
> [18] *And Jesus said unto him, Why callest thou me good? there is none good but one, that is, God.*
> [19] *Thou knowest the commandments, Do not commit adultery, Do not kill, Do not steal, Do not bear false witness, Defraud not, Honour thy father and mother.*
> [20] *And he answered and said unto him, Master, all these have I observed from my youth.*
> [21] *Then Jesus beholding him loved him, and said unto him, One thing thou lackest: go thy way, sell whatsoever thou hast, and give to the poor, and thou shalt have treasure in*

heaven: and come, take up the cross, and follow me.
²² And he was sad at that saying, and went away grieved:
for he had great possessions.

Then, looking around at those that stood nearby, Jesus uttered His words about **how hard it was for those who trusted in their riches to make it into heaven**.

Mark 10:23-25

²³ And Jesus looked round about, and saith unto his disciples, How hardly shall they that have riches enter into the kingdom of God!
²⁴ And the disciples were astonished at his words. But Jesus answereth again, and saith unto them, Children, how hard is it for them that trust in riches to enter into the kingdom of God!
²⁵ It is easier for a camel to go through the eye of a needle, than for a rich man to enter into the kingdom of God.

As Jesus spoke, His disciples were astonished at what He was saying. They could not understand. As they questioned who could possibly be saved, Jesus began to expound to them the power of God.

Mark 10:26-27

²⁶ And they were astonished out of measure, saying among themselves, Who then can be saved?
²⁷ And Jesus looking upon them saith, With men it is impossible, but not with God: for with God all things are possible.

It is not a sin to be rich. Job was a very rich man. However, above his riches, he **trusted in God, and God called Job a perfect and upright** man. Abraham was also a very rich man, yet he **trusted and served the Lord.**

David was also a rich man; he was the King of Israel. He **loved God and asked God to keep him as the apple of His eye.**

Psalm 17:6-8

> [6] *I have called upon thee, for thou wilt hear me, O God: incline thine ear unto me, and hear my speech.*
> [7] *Shew thy marvellous lovingkindness, O thou that savest by thy right hand them which put their trust in thee from those that rise up against them.*
> [8] *Keep me as the apple of the eye, hide me under the shadow of thy wings,*

King David had a very **special relationship with God**. So can we, if we are **willing to pay the price**.

James 1:12

> *Blessed is the man that endureth temptation: for when he is tried, he shall receive the crown of life, which the Lord hath promised to them that love him.*

James begins by saying that "*blessed is the man that endureth temptations*." Blessed to me means *happy is the man*. Why happy? Because we know that **the Lord loves us and cares about us** and what happens to us.

44

Webster's New World College Dictionary defines blessed:

1. enjoying great happiness; blissful
2. bringing comfort or joy

We can truly say that **because we know God, we are blessed**. To know that we are saved, born again, a child of God, that our sins are all forgiven, and that **we have a wonderful home in heaven**, what more could we want?

The apostle Paul wrote to the church at Rome about going through trials and encouraged them. He wanted them to know that **they were blessed, that God would never leave them nor forsake them**.

Romans 8:34-39

34 Who is he that condemneth? It is Christ that died, yea rather, that is risen again, who is even at the right hand of God, who also maketh intercession for us.

35 Who shall separate us from the love of Christ? shall tribulation, or distress, or persecution, or famine, or nakedness, or peril, or sword?

36 As it is written, For thy sake we are killed all the day long; we are accounted as sheep for the slaughter.

37 Nay, in all these things we are more than conquerors through him that loved us.

38 For I am persuaded, that neither death, nor life, nor angels, nor principalities, nor powers, nor things present, nor things to come,

39 Nor height, nor depth, nor any other creature, shall be able to separate us from the love of God, which is in

Christ Jesus our Lord.

The trials and test that we endure, that we go through, these are **all for our benefit**. They make us **strong in the Lord**.

James goes on to say that at the end of this race, this journey, there is laid up for us **a crown of life**, which the Lord Himself shall give to us at the end of this race. Brothers and sisters, **so many great promises are given to us in the pages** of God's Word. We need to take hold of God's promises through His love. In return, we are to **love the Lord even more than we do now**. For it is love that causes us to serve the Lord. It is **love and trust in our Lord and Saviour** that gives us peace in the storm.

This love passes all understanding, for it is a love that **causes us to surrender our will to His** to become His obedient servants. This is a love that we cannot explain, this love that causes us to **weep when we think of all our Saviour** has done for us. We are blessed, oh, how we are blessed.

James 1:13-16

¹³ Let no man say when he is tempted, I am tempted of God: for God cannot be tempted with evil, neither tempteth he any man:
¹⁴ But every man is tempted, when he is drawn away of his own lust, and enticed.
¹⁵ Then when lust hath conceived, it bringeth forth sin: and sin, when it is finished, bringeth forth death.
¹⁶ Do not err, my beloved brethren.

These verses all bear witness to one thing, that **we are all tried and tested**. As we look at the verses and take them one by

46

one, we will see what God wants us to **understand and learn from His Word**. To begin with, we need to understand that **some tests are sent to us from God**. God wants to see **how we will react to the test**. Will we stand by faith and believe God, or will we crumble and fall apart? Will we blame God for what has befallen us?

A mature Christian understands that the trials and tests that befall us are **steppingstones in our overcoming walk with God**. The immature Christian often blames God for their lot in life, for life not being a rose garden. Growing pains are hard on all of us, yet we must **grow in the Lord to be the kind of person** that God desires us to be. These growing pains will not kill us (though we may think so at the time). We must keep on keeping on, for **as we remain true and strong in the Lord, we will overcome and learn**.

Now let us look at these scriptures, beginning with the thirteenth verse: "*Let no man say when he is tempted, I am tempted of God.*" From the days of Adam in the garden unto today, man has tried to blame others for his mistakes and his outright sins. In the garden Eve blamed the serpent, Adam blamed Eve, and then he even blamed God, because God made Eve and gave her to him.

It is, one could say, part of our nature to blame others for our failures. As the world puts it: Everybody passes the buck, but somewhere the buck has to stop. Someone must take the responsibility for the failure. **God does not tempt us.** He does however **test us to see how we will react and hold up** under the pressure of life. It is we, you and I, who let those tests turn into temptations. Of our own lust, we sin and fail God.

In the world today, we live in a society where modern psychology has come up with all kinds of ways for people to blame others for their faults and failures. When it comes to the law, we find numerous ways for guilty people to blame others for their crimes. They blame their parents, their husbands or wives, even their children and society in general for their faults.

A perfect example is when a woman pulls through a drive-through, orders a cup of hot coffee, puts the coffee between her legs, squeezes the cup, burns her legs, and then blames the business where she bought the coffee for her own stupidity. What's worse, she sues the business in court and wins. How stupid can our society get? I am afraid to imagine what lies ahead. Child of God, it is time that we **become what God wants us to** be: a person who **takes responsibility for our actions**. Quit blaming others for your own failures, and do not try to put the blame on God.

Put the blame where it belongs: on Satan and on ourselves. **God is love and goodness.** He may test you, but **He will never tempt you**. James goes on to say: *"for God cannot be tempted with evil, neither tempteth he any man."*

What about 1 Corinthians 10:9, you may ask, where Paul says, *"Neither let us tempt Christ, as some of them also tempted, and were destroyed of serpents."* This does not mean that God was tempted. The Old Testament Israelites pushed God's patience to see what they could get by with. Doing so was a sin, and because of Israel's sin, God brought judgement upon them just as He brings judgement upon sinners today.

I cannot think of any way conceivable that man could tempt the Lord most high. All God did was **bring a righteous and holy judgement upon sinners** who refused to accept God's plan for their lives. When we decide that we are going to do our own thing, and we do not care what God's Word says, then **we can expect God's judgement**.

James 1:14

*But every man is tempted, when he is drawn away of his
own lust, and enticed.*

In verse fourteen James goes on to explain how temptation
works. Temptations come about of our own lust. When we yield
ourselves to our own fleshly desires, temptation comes upon the
scene. I like what Warren Wiersbe has to say about this.

The Wiersbe Bible Commentary: New Testament says:

> The word lust means any kind of desire, and
> not necessarily sexual passions. The normal desires
> of life were given to us by God and, of themselves,
> and are not sinful. Without these desires, we could
> not function. Unless we felt hunger and thirst, we
> would never eat and drink, and we would die.
> Without fatigue, the body would never rest and
> would eventually wear out. Sex is a normal desire;
> without it the human race could not continue.
>
> It is when we want to satisfy these desires in
> ways outside God's will that we get into trouble.
> Eating is normal; gluttony is sin, Sleep is normal;
> laziness is sin. "Marriage is honorable in all, and
> the bed undefiled; but whoremongers and
> adulterers God will judge." (Heb.13:4)

No matter how much we try to blame others, the fault still
lies with us and no one else. I have heard people say, "Well, if
they had not done what they did, then I would not have done what

I did." Regardless, two wrongs never make a right. As I have already said, and will say again, the **desires of life are given to us by God**. These desires are what drive us to **reach our full potential and succeed in life**, and this is perfectly normal. These desires – or lusts, as some would say – are in all of us. When we get angry, temptation comes to us and drives us to angrily lash out. So, what do we do? Do we yield to temptation and lash out, or do we let ourselves **yield to the spirit of God and take control** of the situation?

God will always **make a way of escape in every temptation**. However, we must look for it. We must **take the responsibility for our acts and not blame others**. There are two things we must learn about being tempted.

1. The devil can try and persuade us to give into sin; however, he cannot force us to sin.
2. The old devil can put the bait of sin before us; however, he cannot force us to bite the hook of sin.

Just as when we go fishing, we put the bait on the hook and throw it into the water; however, we cannot make the fish bite. Satan puts the bait before us, the temptation. However, **we make the decision to sin or leave it alone**.

Remember this one thing, when we go fishing, the bait covers or hides the hook, and so it is with temptation. Temptation allures us. It is so pleasing to the eye and to our thoughts. Yet, never forget that **in every temptation there is a hidden hook**. If we bite that hook, **we will be drawn deeper and deeper into sin**. Be not deceived, Satan and the world are not our friends. Satan is the world's best conman. He started in heaven and caused one third of the angels to sin against God. Next, he started in on God's creation of Adam and Eve. Satan appeared to Eve in the form of a serpent. Satan's goal was to deceive Eve and Adam into sinning.

The first thing that Satan does is to bring suggestions to our minds in an attempt to draw our attention, to focus our thoughts on his temptation. Once this is done, he begins to tell us that it won't be so bad just to "try it and see if he's not right." Satan tells us, depending upon the temptation, that it will taste so good or feel so good. Just try it and see for yourself. Surely God won't mind you enjoying some good things in life.

Before long, we begin to listen to what the world is saying. The world tells us that God's Word is wrong and that people need to throw away their Bibles and accept what the world tells us is right. Why? Because the world tries to rationalize everything, and there is no place in a rational world for spirituality. There is no place or need for God.

James 1:15

Then when lust hath conceived, it bringeth forth sin: and sin, when it is finished, bringeth forth death.

In this verse, James describes to us the process of how lust grows and transforms mankind and the final end of that lust. What controls man? His will. **With the will, mankind determines not to sin, or with his will, he says yes to his base desires.** The bait that the devil uses to stir our desires, to allure us, hides the results of sin when it is finished. Thus, blinded by emotions, we do not see the deception that is in front of us. The only thing we see is our desires.

John Phillips gives us a perfect example in his book on James.

The John Phillips Commentary Series says:

> Samson, for example, thought that he could play games with Delilah. She won! She saw him blinded and bound, grinding corn for the Philistines, the sport of his enemies and the mockery of the world. The sin grows in size, it spreads, and it cannot rest until it has others in its coils. No sooner was Eve a sinner than she became a seducer.

This desire, this emotion, when let loose and not controlled, begins to conceive ways of taking the bait that the enemy has put before us. This desire, this will, begins to approve what we have done in our minds. We then reach out and take the bait, and we are hooked like a fish on a line. James warns us that when lust is conceived or is born, that it brings forth sin; and sin when it is finished brings death.

The one thing you must remember is that **it is not a sin to be tempted**; the sin comes when we yield our will to the temptation. Like the old saying goes, you cannot stop the birds from flying over your head, however you **do not have to let them make a nest in your hair**. The soul that sins, it shall die. Sin brings spiritual death, and only **Jesus can bring the dead back to life by His saving grace**.

Eve was the first to sin because she was beguiled by Satan. Adam on the other hand was not deceived. He sinned with full knowledge of what he was doing. By Adam's sin, he plunged all of mankind into a world of sin. The only hope we have is to **yield to God and His saving grace**. We must heed James as he warns us not to err from the way of truth.

James 1:17

Every good gift and every perfect gift is from above, and cometh down from the Father of lights, with whom is no variableness, neither shadow of turning.

The very first thing man needs to understand is that **God is unchangeable in His righteousness**. God is holy and can bear no evil in His presence. Scripture states that **every good and perfect gift comes from our heavenly Father** which is above. God is good and all His gifts are good and perfect to us ward. God **wishes only good for us**, though at times, because of our sin and trespasses or bad conduct, God must bring judgement upon us to bring us back to our senses.

God's love for man has been from the very beginning, from the day of creation. It has **never wavered toward those who love Him**. When all of mankind turned their backs on God except for Noah and his family, God destroyed them all, yet made a way of escape for the eight souls that loved Him. God, the great Father of Lights, is **forever the same, unchangeable in His holiness**.

James 1:18

Of his own will begat he us with the word of truth, that we should be a kind of firstfruits of his creatures.

James in this verse is **giving us a look at the new birth** from his point of view. Salvation is a **gift from God**. James expresses that salvation came as a result of God's own will and desire. Jesus, God's own Son, became the **supreme sacrifice for sin, the last and final sacrifice**. What the blood of bulls, lambs and goats could not do, the blood of Jesus did. *"That we should be a kind of firstfruits of his creatures."*

Jesus brought to man a salvation that **broke all the old laws**. No longer was man separated from God by a veil. We are **given access to the Kingdom of God**. No longer was a priesthood needed to stand between God and man. **We can go straight to God with our needs and petitions.** Oh, how God loves us.

Romans 11:16-23

16 For if the firstfruit be holy, the lump is also holy: and if the root be holy, so are the branches.

17 And if some of the branches be broken off, and thou, being a wild olive tree, wert graffed in among them, and with them partakest of the root and fatness of the olive tree;

18 Boast not against the branches. But if thou boast, thou bearest not the root, but the root thee.

19 Thou wilt say then, The branches were broken off, that I might be graffed in.

20 Well; because of unbelief they were broken off, and thou standest by faith. Be not highminded, but fear:

21 For if God spared not the natural branches, take heed lest he also spare not thee.

22 Behold therefore the goodness and severity of God: on them which fell, severity; but toward thee, goodness, if thou continue in his goodness: otherwise thou also shalt be cut off.

23 And they also, if they abide not still in unbelief, shall be graffed in: for God is able to graff them in again.

1 Corinthians 15:19-23

¹⁹ If in this life only we have hope in Christ, we are of all men most miserable.
²⁰ But now is Christ risen from the dead, and become the firstfruits of them that slept.
²¹ For since by man came death, by man came also the resurrection of the dead.
²² For as in Adam all die, even so in Christ shall all be made alive.
²³ But every man in his own order: Christ the firstfruits; afterward they that are Christ's at his coming.

These scriptures tell us that if we will listen to what God is saying, we'll **learn the wonderful things God does for us**. The plan of salvation **comes through Jesus and His blood**. Through Jesus, we, the Gentiles, are offered salvation through faith. Faith in Jesus and His shed blood **washes away a multitude of sins**.

But sadly, too many people do not seem to understand what God is saying to us. Even in our churches, too many people never seem to grow, never seem to rise above their starting point.

Church, **God's desire is for us to grow**, to spiritually increase. I have heard people pray (and I have prayed myself): "Lord, more of thee and less of me." The question is whether they (and you) understand that **for the Lord to increase, we must decrease**. I have said this before and will say it over and over, praying that you will understand. If we will give ourselves over to Jesus, we will be **blessed and victorious in life**.

Brothers and sisters, too many times we cannot see the

forest because of all the trees. I am saying that we need to look at the big picture and not at the few things around us. At the creation, at the time Adam and Eve were created, God, Jesus and the Holy Ghost knew that **there was coming a day when Jesus would be crucified** on the cross for the sins of mankind. In Revelation 13:8, the Bible speaks of Jesus as *"the Lamb slain from the foundation of the world."*

In the foreknowledge of God, He **knew what was going to happen**. He knew that there was coming a time when there would be **a day of redemption for man**. The price was great; however, it was the only way to give all of Adam's descendants a chance to make heaven their home and to come into the **fellowship that God wanted from the beginning**. I hope that you can feel my concern for the lost souls of the world.

We must preach and teach **Jesus Christ crucified as the only hope** for the lost. The enemy hates us and seeks to bring us down, and he is doing a good job of it. In these United States of America, our government is trying to turn the people of this nation against the churches of God and against the Christian people who believe in living a pleasing life before God. May God save us from ourselves.

This nation, regardless of what popular opinion says, was **founded upon religious and personal freedom**. It is sad when the rights of the few outweigh the rights of the many. Our government has repeatedly struggled with adhering to the principles of our founding fathers. And now our government is trying to dictate morality to the churches of the living God and to tell us what we should believe and not believe.

Take heart, my brothers and sisters, for **God is still on the throne**, and like it or not, **He is in control**. We must surrender ourselves to the Lord and His service. It is time for the churches to **stand up for what is right and to denounce evil in all of its forms**, regardless of what people will think or say. Trust in God, for **He will always make a way for His loving children**.

James 1:19-20

19 Wherefore, my beloved brethren, let every man be swift to hear, slow to speak, slow to wrath:
20 For the wrath of man worketh not the righteousness of God.

James in these verses is exhorting us to be **quick to hear, slow to speak, and slow to wrath**. When we get to verse twenty-one, we will look at what James calls the ingrafted word. We as the saved, born-again Christian **receive the spirit of Christ at salvation**. Along with accepting Jesus as our Saviour, we also accept God's Word as the **authority in our lives**. God's Word makes changes in us as we yield ourselves to His sovereignty, spiritual changes as well as natural changes. It changes how we **act and interact with those around us**, how we think and how we talk with those around us. It **changes our character from the inside and the outside**. What a difference Jesus makes in the hearts of believers!

One thing Christians are good at is getting used to what goes on around us and hearing what we want to hear. Years ago, I worked in a very noisy place. I became so accustomed to the noise that when any one part of that sound changed, I instantly knew it. It is very important that we, as Christians, **train ourselves to hear and know the voice of God**, so that if His voice changes, we know it. In 1 Kings, chapter nineteen, verse nine, God spoke to Elijah. Elijah was hiding in a cave and God asked Elijah: "*What* *doest thou here, Elijah?"* Elijah gave God his reasons for hiding; however, God was not satisfied and told Elijah to **go and stand out on the mountain**.

The scripture states in verse eleven that **the Lord passed by**. There was a strong wind, and it rent the mountains and broke the rocks into pieces before the Lord; however, the Lord was not in the wind. After the wind there was an earthquake, but the Lord was not in the earthquake. Then after the earthquake, there was a fire, and the Lord was not in the fire. However, after the fire, **there was a still small voice, and Elijah knew that it was the Lord**.

1 Kings 19:9-13

⁹ And he came thither unto a cave, and lodged there; and, behold, the word of the LORD came to him, and he said unto him, What doest thou here, Elijah?
¹⁰ And he said, I have been very jealous for the LORD God of hosts: for the children of Israel have forsaken thy covenant, thrown down thine altars, and slain thy prophets with the sword; and I, even I only, am left; and they seek my life, to take it away.
¹¹ And he said, Go forth, and stand upon the mount before the LORD. And, behold, the LORD passed by, and a great and strong wind rent the mountains, and brake in pieces the rocks before the LORD; but the LORD was not in the wind: and after the wind an earthquake; but the LORD was not in the earthquake:
¹² And after the earthquake a fire; but the LORD was not in the fire: and after the fire a still small voice.
¹³ And it was so, when Elijah heard it, that he wrapped his

face in his mantle, and went out, and stood in the entering
in of the cave. And, behold, there came a voice unto him,
and said, What doest thou here, Elijah?

Elijah learned what we all must learn. He learned to **listen and know the voice of the Lord**. Saints today, the Lord is still speaking, although not many are learning to listen. So many people are missing out on so much because they refuse to listen to the voice of God. We should be constantly praying that God will somehow **break down the barriers that bind lost souls**. That He will take sleep from their eyes, and that He will give them no rest or peace until they **fall before Him and repent of their sins**. That He will speak to them in that still, small voice of His glory, power and peace.

To make heaven our home, we must **learn to listen and know the voice** of our Lord.

Psalm 95:6-7

⁶ O come, let us worship and bow down: let us kneel
before the LORD our maker.
⁷ For he is our God; and we are the people of his pasture,
and the sheep of his hand. To day if ye will hear his voice,

Hebrews 3:7-8

⁷ Wherefore (as the Holy Ghost saith, To day if ye will
hear his voice,
⁸ Harden not your hearts, as in the provocation, in the day
of temptation in the wilderness:

John 10:1-5

¹ Verily, verily, I say unto you, He that entereth not by the door into the sheepfold, but climbeth up some other way, the same is a thief and a robber.

² But he that entereth in by the door is the shepherd of the sheep.

³ To him the porter openeth; and the sheep hear his voice: and he calleth his own sheep by name, and leadeth them out.

⁴ And when he putteth forth his own sheep, he goeth before them, and the sheep follow him: for they know his voice.

⁵ And a stranger will they not follow, but will flee from him: for they know not the voice of strangers.

These scriptures teach us that it is vital that the child of God **knows His voice and follows Him**. If we do not know that we are saved (born again), it is because we are not saved. When a person gets saved, they know it because there **is a change that takes place** inside of them. No change, no salvation. It is as simple as that. The old man of sin must depart, and **in his place stands a new man in Christ Jesus**.

I use the following example often in my writings and preaching because it happened to me. I worked with a young lady, and she was having a bad day. It seemed things were not going right for her. She was complaining and using some very bad language. I began to talk to her and told her that if she would **give her heart and life to Jesus and get saved, things would be bette**r, whereupon she told me she was saved. I asked her what she was saved from. She told me, "Well, I don't know. But my pastor told me that I was saved."

This happens all too often in churches today. We can only see the outward fruits, not the inner heart. The pastor tells people that they are saved, yet no evidence of change takes place. It is vital to never tell someone they are saved. If they cannot tell, most likely there has been no change in their heart.

One of my pet peeves is when I hear (or hear of) a preacher telling someone that they are called into the ministry. If you are called into the ministry, **God will tell you, not the preacher**. Preachers who do this are setting that person up for failure. If God does not call them, without that God-given call, they will never succeed in the true ministry. One of the problems today in the church world is that there are too many ministers who have never been called by God. Please forgive me. I digress.

Another thing we must learn to do is **be slow to speak**. Too many times we **speak before we think about what we are really saying**. We must remember that once something is said, it **can never be unsaid**; and too many times it will come back to haunt us throughout the rest of our lives.

A perfect example comes from the world of politics. We have seen many politicians drop out of elections or lose elections because of something they said or did years before. Words have power. **They can kill or give life by how we use them.** King David in Psalms 39:1 speaks of being careful with what we say because a man can show his wisdom or his foolishness by the things he speaks. Solomon also says **a man should be careful with what he speaks**.

Psalm 39:1

I said, I will take heed to my ways, that I sin not with my

61

tongue: I will keep my mouth with a bridle, while the wicked is before me.

Proverbs 10:19-20

[19] In the multitude of words there wanteth not sin: but he that refraineth his lips is wise.
[20] The tongue of the just is as choice silver: the heart of the wicked is little worth.

Proverbs 21:23

Whoso keepeth his mouth and his tongue keepeth his soul from troubles.

Remember, **he that bridles his tongue is wise**.

In the final part of verse nineteen, James speaks of being slow to wrath. Then, in verse twenty, he gives us the reason why. We have seen individuals who are quick to lose their temper, or as the world says, they fly off the handle at the least things. These types of people have very little self-control. Anger that is not controlled is very dangerous and gives no glory to God. **The Word tells us to anger and sin not.**

There are times we cannot help but get mad at something or someone around us. Yet, God's Word tells us **not to let that anger cause us to sin**. Remember, the world is watching us and they would love nothing better than to catch us losing control. We are **living this life and running this race to please God**. We are to **give praise and glory to our Lord**. We are to give it by our voice and by the way that we live. Our lives are to be **a witness before this lost and dying world**. Let everything we do be to the glory of God and His righteousness.

Let your life be a light that **shines in this present darkness**. Souls are at stake.

James 1:21-22

²¹ Wherefore lay apart all filthiness and superfluity of naughtiness, and receive with meekness the engrafted word, which is able to save your souls.
²² But be ye doers of the word, and not hearers only, deceiving your own selves.

James makes the point in this twenty-first verse that to serve the Lord, there are some things we must do. He speaks of **laying aside all filthiness and superfluity of naughtiness**. Then receive with meekness the ingrafted Word of God that is able to **bring salvation to the soul**. I can hear some of you say, "I thought we are saved by grace through the blood of Jesus Christ." Yes, we are. However, the Word of God teaches us **how to *stay* saved**.

Salvation **is a gift from God**, but like anything we possess, **we can keep it, lose it, or throw it away**. Many people have the misguided idea that once salvation is given to us by God, it is ours with no cost to us. They are wrong in this kind of thinking.

Let us go to what Jesus said in the parable of the sower.

Matthew 13:3-9

³ And he spake many things unto them in parables, saying, Behold, a sower went forth to sow;
⁴ And when he sowed, some seeds fell by the way side, and

the fowls came and devoured them up:

⁵ Some fell upon stony places, where they had not much earth: and forthwith they sprung up, because they had no deepness of earth:

⁶ And when the sun was up, they were scorched; and because they had no root, they withered away.

⁷ And some fell among thorns; and the thorns sprung up, and choked them:

⁸ But other fell into good ground, and brought forth fruit, some an hundredfold, some sixtyfold, some thirtyfold.

⁹ Who hath ears to hear, let him hear.

Jesus speaks of a man going out to sow seed in his field. As he sowed his seed, some seeds fell by the wayside, and the birds came and ate them. Some fell upon stony places and began to grow. Because the dirt was shallow, the heat of the sun scorched them and they died. Some seed fell among thorny places and was choked out and unfruitful. Some fell upon good ground and brought forth much grain.

After this, the disciples asked Jesus why He spoke to the people in parables. He told them that **they were to know the mysteries of heaven but not the common people, not yet.** They were to be the **founding fathers of the coming church**, although they did not yet know it.

Matthew 13:10-17

¹⁰ And the disciples came, and said unto him, Why speakest thou unto them in parables?

¹¹ He answered and said unto them, Because it is given unto you to know the mysteries of the kingdom of heaven, but to them it is not given.

[12] For whosoever hath, to him shall be given, and he shall have more abundance: but whosoever hath not, from him shall be taken away even that he hath.

[13] Therefore speak I to them in parables: because they seeing see not; and hearing they hear not, neither do they understand.

[14] And in them is fulfilled the prophecy of Esaias, which saith, By hearing ye shall hear, and shall not understand; and seeing ye shall see, and shall not perceive:

[15] For this people's heart is waxed gross, and their ears are dull of hearing, and their eyes they have closed; lest at any time they should see with their eyes, and hear with their ears, and should understand with their heart, and should be converted, and I should heal them.

[16] But blessed are your eyes, for they see: and your ears, for they hear.

[17] For verily I say unto you, That many prophets and righteous men have desired to see those things which ye see, and have not seen them; and to hear those things which ye hear, and have not heard them.

It seems not very much has changed. We now have the **pure Word of God at our disposal** to read and study. We have **Bible classes and the preaching** of the Word. Still, we have people hearing, yet they do not hear; and seeing, they do not see. Too many times we have the blind trying to lead the blind. Over and over I hear people say, "I read the Bible; however, I cannot understand it." To them I say, "You cannot read the Bible like you read any other book. You must pray and **ask God to reveal the truth of His Word** to you." Nevertheless, people do not want to take the time for God to do this for them.

They are like my dad. When we went fishing, if the fish did not bite within five to ten minutes, he was ready to go. In serving God and studying His Word, we must be willing to **take the time for God to do the work** within us. If we take time for God, we will **hear and understand**, and understanding God will **give us the spirit of understanding**.

Jesus then begins to give to His disciples the meaning of the parable of the sower.

Matthew 13:18-23

[18] Hear ye therefore the parable of the sower.
[19] When any one heareth the word of the kingdom, and understandeth it not, then cometh the wicked one, and catcheth away that which was sown in his heart. This is he which received seed by the way side.
[20] But he that received the seed into stony places, the same is he that heareth the word, and anon with joy receiveth it;
[21] Yet hath he not root in himself, but dureth for a while: for when tribulation or persecution ariseth because of the word, by and by he is offended.
[22] He also that received seed among the thorns is he that heareth the word; and the care of this world, and the deceitfulness of riches, choke the word, and he becometh unfruitful.
[23] But he that received seed into the good ground is he that heareth the word, and understandeth it; which also beareth fruit, and bringeth forth, some an hundredfold, some sixty, some thirty.

As we look at what Jesus is saying, everything is perfectly clear. The seed that fell by the wayside is the true Word of God, the gospel. How many times have we been in church services and seen people reject the gospel message and walk away, as lost as they came?

Then Jesus speaks of the seed falling upon stony ground. These are people who hear the gospel message, accept it with joy and give their hearts to Jesus as Lord. Jesus goes on to say that because there is no effort to grow, to establish a relationship with Him as the Lord of their lives, to be anchored in the Word, when trials and tribulations or persecutions come against them, they lose heart and become disillusioned. Little by little they begin to give up on God and walk away. Even though they profess Christ, they fail in their relationship with Him.

2 Thessalonians 2:10-12

> *[10] And with all deceivableness of unrighteousness in them that perish; because they received not the love of the truth, that they might be saved.*
> *[11] And for this cause God shall send them strong delusion, that they should believe a lie:*
> *[12] That they all might be damned who believed not the truth, but had pleasure in unrighteousness.*

Contrary to what many believe and many denominations teach, **these people were genuine Christians**. Jesus tells us they **received the Word with joy**. This tells us very plainly that they **were saved, or born again**. I realize there are many who will say they were never really saved, or they would have stayed in church. However, I'm telling you that we should withhold

67

judgement of others until we have walked in their shoes.

Then there is another group who believe that when we get saved, our soul is forever saved no matter what we do or say. A person can be a liar, adulterer, take God's name in vain, be a drunkard and still be saved. That they will go to heaven anyway. This is contrary to the Word of God. For too long we have been trying to make God's Word say what we want it to say. **We must take the Word to mean what it says, for His Word is the final authority.**

In verse twenty-two, we have an example similar to verse twenty. Here, the gospel falls among the thorns, weeds we can say, and before too long, the young Christian is beset by the cares of life. The deceit of this world chokes them in their walk with God, and they become unfruitful and spiritually die. **Yes, these, too, were saved.**

Finally, Jesus speaks of the seed falling on good ground. What is the difference? The good ground is **where people have a made-up mind that they are going to live for God**. They pray, read and study their Bible so that they may be pleasing to God. When trials come their way, they **go to God in prayer**. They stand upon God's Word because God's Word is our final authority. In this way, they **remain strong in God and do not backslide**.

Can a man backslide and become a castaway? Yes, he can. Even Paul writes of it in 1 Corinthians.

1 Corinthians 9:27

But I keep under my body, and bring it into subjection: lest that by any means, when I have preached to others, I myself should be a castaway.

68

How do we become a castaway? When we stop praying, stop reading, and stop studying God's Word. When we stop doing these things, we begin to grow cold within our souls. We get weaker and weaker and finally we die spiritually. The best way to stay alive spiritually is to **do as the Bible tells us**, to **receive with meekness the ingrafted Word of God**.

The Bible speaks of the wild olive branch being grafted into the vine. We are that wild olive branch that has been **brought into the family of God**. Until Jesus died upon the cross, we were outcast. Lost without any hope. However, through the precious blood of Jesus, we were **grafted into the family of God**. Our future was changed. There **flowed within us the power and presence of God**, something that we had never had before.

We are now spiritually alive; the spirit of Christ dwells within us. As we read and study our Bibles, **God's Holy Word becomes part of us**. It finds lodging in our hearts and minds and **teaches us how to walk with the Lord Jesus**.

James 1:23-24

23 For if any be a hearer of the word, and not a doer, he is like unto a man beholding his natural face in a glass:
24 For he beholdeth himself, and goeth his way, and straightway forgetteth what manner of man he was.

As we look at this twenty-third verse, James is giving us yet again another illustration of how foolish men can be and often are. James is stressing that to please God, it is not enough to be a hearer of the gospel, but **we must be a doer of the gospel**. I have found in my years as a minister and pastor that people have many misconceived ideas.

One of these ideas is that we go to church to serve God. This is wrong thinking. We do not go to church to serve God. We go to church to **learn how to serve God**. We hear teachers and preachers expound on the Word of God. However, it is of no use to us until **we put into practice what we have learned** and heard. God's desire is to **bless us and anoint us as we go forward** in His service. It is not enough just to hear. In the workplace we receive instruction on how to do certain jobs. After the instruction is over, the employers expect their employees to go and do the work. The reward is to be paid for the job well done. It is the same way with God **if we follow His instructions in the Word**. Then we are **blessed in every aspect** of our lives.

James speaks to us in these verses and explains that a man who is a hearer of the Word and not a doer is like a man who looks at himself in a mirror, walks away, and immediately forgets what he looks like. Child of God, **there is a work that must be done, and we all have our parts** to do. If everyone will do their part, then we will **see the glory of God manifested** and the victory won.

The idea that we can "let someone else do it" will not bring victory to us. So, let us **roll up our sleeves and get to the work** that is set before us.

James 1:25-27

²⁵ But whoso looketh into the perfect law of liberty, and continueth therein, he being not a forgetful hearer, but a doer of the work, this man shall be blessed in his deed. ²⁶ If any man among you seem to be religious, and bridleth not his tongue, but deceiveth his own heart, this man's religion is vain.

70

*²⁷ Pure religion and undefiled before God and the Father
is this, To visit the fatherless and widows in their
affliction, and to keep himself unspotted from the world.*

James goes on to express that the man or woman who **looks into or studies the Word of God** will be **blessed in all that they do**. When we search God's perfect law for our lives, we **find what we have been looking for** to make us complete. The Word of God as we study it begins to make changes, both **within us and on the outside**.

God's Word perfects us and **makes our lives into what God wants them to be**. Under the law, everything was laid out for God's people. The rules were set and followed. When Jesus died on the cross, the **era of grace was established**. The blood of Jesus replaced the law, and **grace was given unto people everywhere**. As we take the advantage of studying God's Holy Word and living by what we have learned, we are **blessed and refreshed by God**.

Studying God's Word is like looking into a mirror. In the Word, **we can see what God wants us to be**, and it also shows us what we are truly like. We can see our faults and our failures, and we can **see how far we still have to go**. However, God is loving and patient, and **as long as we are striving to reach that perfection in Him, God will work with us**.

I don't want you misled. **Our God is loving and patient, but his laws are still in effect.** We no longer live under the law of blood sacrifice or the rabbinical law, but laws such as the **Ten Commandments** (do not steal; do not lie; do not commit adultery; and all of the others) **still apply to each of us**. Then there are other sins listed in the Word. If you allow them to become part of your life, they will keep you out of the Kingdom of Heaven. The scriptures below give you a part of what these sins are.

Matthew 7:21-23

21 Not every one that saith unto me, Lord, Lord, shall enter into the kingdom of heaven; but he that doeth the will of my Father which is in heaven.
22 Many will say to me in that day, Lord, Lord, have we not prophesied in thy name? and in thy name have cast out devils? and in thy name done many wonderful works?
23 And then will I profess unto them, I never knew you: depart from me, ye that work iniquity.

Romans 1:21-32

21 Because that, when they knew God, they glorified him not as God, neither were thankful; but became vain in their imaginations, and their foolish heart was darkened.
22 Professing themselves to be wise, they became fools,
23 And changed the glory of the uncorruptible God into an image made like to corruptible man, and to birds, and fourfooted beasts, and creeping things.
24 Wherefore God also gave them up to uncleanness through the lusts of their own hearts, to dishonour their own bodies between themselves:
25 Who changed the truth of God into a lie, and worshipped and served the creature more than the Creator, who is blessed for ever. Amen.
26 For this cause God gave them up unto vile affections: for even their women did change the natural use into that which is against nature:

[27]{.superscript} And likewise also the men, leaving the natural use of the woman, burned in their lust one toward another; men with men working that which is unseemly, and receiving in themselves that recompence of their error which was meet.

[28] And even as they did not like to retain God in their knowledge, God gave them over to a reprobate mind, to do those things which are not convenient;

[29] Being filled with all unrighteousness, fornication, wickedness, covetousness, maliciousness; full of envy, murder, debate, deceit, malignity; whisperers,

[30] Backbiters, haters of God, despiteful, proud, boasters, inventors of evil things, disobedient to parents,

[31] Without understanding, covenantbreakers, without natural affection, implacable, unmerciful:

[32] Who knowing the judgment of God, that they which commit such things are worthy of death, not only do the same, but have pleasure in them that do them.

Galatians 5:19-21

[19] Now the works of the flesh are manifest, which are these; Adultery, fornication, uncleanness, lasciviousness,

[20] Idolatry, witchcraft, hatred, variance, emulations, wrath, strife, seditions, heresies,

[21] Envyings, murders, drunkenness, revellings, and such like: of the which I tell you before, as I have also told you in time past, that they which do such things shall not inherit the kingdom of God.

Revelation 21:8

But the fearful, and unbelieving, and the abominable, and

murderers, and whoremongers, and sorcerers, and idolaters, and all liars, shall have their part in the lake which burneth with fire and brimstone: which is the second death.

The mirror of God's Word will keep us from all these things listed above. Child of God, when we get involved in the sins of this world, it closes off the door to heaven. **Straight is the gate and narrow is the way that leads to eternal life.**

Matthew 7:13-14

[13] Enter ye in at the strait gate: for wide is the gate, and broad is the way, that leadeth to destruction, and many there be which go in thereat:
[14] Because strait is the gate, and narrow is the way, which leadeth unto life, and few there be that find it.

In verse twenty-six, James talks about people who seem to be religious, but they let the flesh take control of them. What is religion? **Religion is the outward show of serving God**; however, too many times people only have an outward show, while inside they are spiritually dead.

Jesus did not come to start a new religion. He came to bring **a spiritual relationship with God**. The Jews had a religion, a religion that could not bring a relationship with God. Man needed to be able to **touch and feel the power of God**. Yes, in the Old Testament, there were a few who reached that place. However, only a few. The presence of God and His power **needed to be experienced by everyone**. This was why Jesus came and died, to **remove the veil that hid God from mankind**.

A perfect example of religion is when we look at Judaism, with the priesthood, the scribes and the Pharisees of the Old Testament. As a rule, we can label something as a religion when it is dead, dry and lifeless. **Christianity is much more.** It is a glorious relationship with God. What makes Christianity so different? It is because at salvation, the **spirit of Jesus Christ comes into our hearts to live in us** and through us. In our own power there is no way possible that we can live this Christian life. Yet, when Jesus comes in, and we yield our lives to Him, **He lives through us and God receives praise and glory**. We are indwelled by the very presence of Jesus Christ.

There are far too many people today who have religion. They do not have a born-again experience with God. They trust in church membership for salvation. They trust in water baptism. These cannot save a person. **There must be more.** There has to be that **personal touch from the Master**, that **everyday relationship with Jesus**. Without it we are lifeless. All we have is a form of godliness, but no power.

James gives us an example, an illustration, if you will, of a person who professes to being a Christian. He has no control and lashes out at those around him. He speaks words that should not be said. How many of us know the same kind of people as this man? When they get mad, they curse and say all kinds of ungodly things. Yet they profess to being good Christians. As James states, they are only fooling themselves by trying to hide the fact that they are not where they should be with the Lord. Their profession is false; their religion is in vain. Their witness is destroyed.

In verse twenty-seven, James summarizes **what he considers to be true religion, true salvation**, how Christians should conduct themselves before the world: *"pure religion and undefiled before God and the Father is this, To visit the fatherless* and widows in their affliction." The children of God must **give of themselves to those who are in need**. God calls upon us to be His hand extended, to **visit the sick and the needy**, to pray for the sick and those suffering afflictions. We are to **plead for the lost that they may be saved**, and to pray for our fellow Christians, **holding them up before God**. Our duty is to pray for His church, and **to be faithful to the Lord**. We read in Matthew the following:

Matthew 25:34-40

> *34 Then shall the King say unto them on his right hand, Come, ye blessed of my Father, inherit the kingdom prepared for you from the foundation of the world:*
> *35 For I was an hungred, and ye gave me meat: I was thirsty, and ye gave me drink: I was a stranger, and ye took me in:*
> *36 Naked, and ye clothed me: I was sick, and ye visited me: I was in prison, and ye came unto me.*
> *37 Then shall the righteous answer him, saying, Lord, when saw we thee an hungred, and fed thee? or thirsty, and gave thee drink?*
> *38 When saw we thee a stranger, and took thee in? or naked, and clothed thee?*
> *39 Or when saw we thee sick, or in prison, and came unto thee?*
> *40 And the King shall answer and say unto them, Verily I say unto you, Inasmuch as ye have done it unto one of the least of these my brethren, ye have done it unto me.*

These are the words of Jesus, my friend. How do you

measure up to what Jesus is saying here? James closes out this twenty-seventh verse by saying that **the true child of God will keep unspotted from the world**. The stains of sin were **washed away when we were saved**. Now we must do **whatever is necessary to stay free** from the stains of sin.

Chapter 1 Review Questions

1. What was James relationship to Jesus?

_____

_____

_____

2. In Galatians, Paul states that he went to Jerusalem and stayed

with Peter. While he was there, who else did he see?

_____

_____

_____

3. There is no record of James's death in the Bible. Where can

you find a record of his death?

_____

_____

4. How did James die?

_____

_____

_____

5. To whom was the book of James written?

_____

_____

6. What must we learn to be, before we can be a good leader?

_____

_____

_____

7. To be of any use to the Lord we must first become . . .

_____

_____

8. Trials are a part of the believer's life. What do they do for us?

_____

_____

_____

9. What must we show God first if we want to receive anything

from Him?

_____

_____

10. What are we showing when we second guess everything?

_____

_____

_____

11. What do the churches today have in common with the churches in the days of James?

_____

_____

_____

12. At the end of this race, this journey, there waits for us a . . .

_____

_____

_____

13. When we are tried and tested, from whom do these trials and tests come?

_____

_____

_____

14. Where do the temptations that we go through come from?

_____

_____

_____

15. Who blamed whom in the garden because of sin?

_____

_____

16. No matter how much we try to put the blame on others, the

_____

_____

17. What are the two things we must learn about being tempted?

_____

_____

_____

18. What controls man?

_____

_____

_____

19. What were the Gentiles offered through Jesus?

_____

_____

_____

20. For the Lord to increase we must first . . .

_____

_____

21. What is important for us to learn, to listen to and to know?

_____

_____

_____

22. Remember this, that once something is said it can . . .

_____

_____

23. If we take the time for God, then we will hear and understand.

We will read and understand because . . .

_____

_____

24. We do not go to church to serve God; we go to . . .

_____

_____

25. As we study God's Word, it is like looking into a mirror.

What do we see in the Word of God?

_____

_____

_____

Chapter 2

The Bible is full of teachings on how mature Christians **are to live and conduct themselves**. Sadly, most of the Christian world does not live according to what the Bible teaches. There are two main groups with variants in between. One group is the fundamentalists who **believe in the literal truth of the Bible**. The other faction is the liberals who **consider themselves to be open minded**, favoring progressive ideals, and who do away with the basic truths of the Bible in favor of a very permissive religion.

I do not know to which group you belong. However, I can tell you that **the Bible is the living Word of God, and it is forever established**. It cannot be changed regardless of what men and women say or do. It will forever remain the same.

A devilish trend today is trying to change the meaning of God's Word. Nothing liberal Christians say or do will change what God has established. When the Bible says that **certain things are sin, then they are forever a sin**, no matter what people may say, even the so-called church. The trend of the liberal church movement is to change their doctrinal statements and views to go along with the popular opinions of the people, or the masses.

They have completely forgotten that on judgement day

God will judge everyone by His established Word, not by their diluted church dogmas or philosophical ideals. Many church denominations today are changing their doctrinal statements and beliefs in an attempt to keep or hold on to the people in their churches. The only thing I know of that will keep people from leaving churches today **is a mighty move of God's spirit**. They need to quit programming God out of their services. The church must have **God's spirit working in every part of the church**, from the preaching, to the teaching, to the youth ministry. **God's spirit must be in every part of the church.** When we let God's spirit move in our churches, people will **get in and move with God**.

James 2:1

My brethren, have not the faith of our Lord Jesus Christ, the Lord of glory, with respect of persons.

James in this first verse of the second chapter writes about how we are **not to have respect of persons**, or to show favoritism. Much has been said about how James worded this verse. What was James trying to say? He was saying that if we have the faith of Jesus Christ our Lord, then we will be obedient to the teachings of Christ and **not have respect of persons in our heart and life**. Jesus taught that if we play the partiality game, then we are out of the will of God. As we study the teachings of Jesus and the apostles, they teach us that **God is not concerned about whether you are rich or poor, man or woman, your racial status or your color**. God looks at the heart, for His desire is that **all should be saved**. We, like Jesus, need to show the same spirit of love to everyone we meet. If we show **love, genuine love, to**

86

those around us, then we show forth the spirit of Christ.

We can look down through history and see where favoritism and partiality plus prejudice have led to wars and to rioting. Because of skin color or ethnic background, many have been tortured, put into prison, or killed. To me, the worst is because of their religious beliefs. It has been said that more wars have been fought over religion than any other cause. Man's inhumanity towards man, one person's hate for another who does not meet his preconceived ideas, is beyond measure.

For example, when Hitler became head of the German government, he began to preach a doctrine of hate against other races. Every race of people was inferior to the German or Aryan people. Hitler wanted a pure Aryan race of blond-headed, blue-eyed people. To achieve his goal of German superiority, he began by poisoning people's minds against the Jewish people. Then Hitler started stirring the same hatred against the Polish people. In the end, not counting the millions killed in bombings and fighting on the ground, he killed six million Jews in the death camps alone. No one knows how many other races died there. On top of the death camps, hundreds of thousands died in slave labor camps. This is what happens when you preach hate and prejudice.

Man is not naturally prejudiced. He is taught to be intolerant and bigoted toward others. He is trained to be prejudiced about the color of a person's skin, prejudiced concerning rich verses poor, or socially prejudiced about who is acceptable or not to sit at his table. If you do not fit into their mold, their preconceived ideas, then they want nothing to do with you. How degrading man can be to his fellow man!

However, praise God, **Jesus is not that way**. He makes **no distinction between man and woman, rich or poor**. The main thing that Jesus looks at is the heart of an individual. Jesus was honest with everyone, for unlike man, He **did not and does not lie** to anyone. Prejudices are bad enough; however, when they are in the church, they cause terrible problems. If the pastor of a church shows partiality to some of his church members, he is asking for trouble.

I saw this growing up in our local church. One family asked the pastor out for dinner quite a lot. The pastor and his wife were **pleased to be asked out, so they happily agreed**. Other church members felt ignored, saying the pastor felt some in the church were of less worth than others who "had the money to wine and dine the pastor." The pastor was **not prejudiced toward those less financially blessed**; however, a few folks got it into their minds that he was, and the tongues began to wag, causing problems over nothing. Finally, the pastor told the whole church that if they did not like him and his wife going out to eat with this certain family, "Then you need to invite us to your home for dinner or invite us to go out with you." His response pretty much solved the problem. Strangely, hardly anyone invited the pastor and his wife out to eat with them except the same family as before the trouble started.

Saints, my advice is to **not get bent out of shape about anything so unimportant**. If you are upset about something, talk to the pastor, if need be. Then be prepared to **do whatever is necessary to remedy the problem**. Whatever you do, **do it in a Christ-like manner**. We must do all to the glory of God. Saints, gossip and rumors do nothing but stir up trouble, usually about nothing.

In one of the churches we pastored, I had a man come to me and tell me he felt like we needed to start a bus ministry. I told the brother that it was **a great idea and that I would get him a bus**. He said, "Oh, I did not mean for me to do it." Whereupon I informed him, "Brother, the **Lord laid it upon your heart, not mine**. Therefore, do you not think that **since God gave you the vision, you are the one** to do the work?"

There is always someone who is willing to volunteer others for different jobs in the church. If you feel that a certain thing needs to be done in the church, then **talk to the pastor and see if you can do it yourself**. Do not volunteer others. **Do what God has shown you needs to be done.** Do it yourself. Please God and surprise your pastor. He might even faint.

We need that Christ-like spirit in us that we might **let others see Jesus in us**. A person's soul is the **most precious thing they possess**. Our prejudices turn people away from our God and the church. Sinners have a preconceived idea of how Christians should act. They believe that we are not to voice our opinions; we are not to stand up for what we believe; we are to let everyone run over us. They have fallen for the devil's lies and blame Christians for the world's woes. As sinners, they are headed for an eternity without God. They have the idea that if they do not believe in God, then they are not accountable to God for their actions. The devil's lie is working very well in the hearts of this world. When you do away with the biblical concept of creation, you have done away with God in their minds.

The prejudices that the world holds causes them to judge the churches as racist and as prejudiced bigots. Why? Because the saints of God **hold to the standards of righteousness and holiness**, and the world hates this with a passion. The world demands that we believe what they tell us to believe and act the way they think we should. However, the true child of God **desires to be like Jesus**. Remember, our goal to be Christ-like and to live a life where **the world does not see us**. Instead, they see **Jesus in us**.

James 2:2-4

² For if there come unto your assembly a man with a gold ring, in goodly apparel, and there come in also a poor man in vile raiment;
³ And ye have respect to him that weareth the gay clothing, and say unto him, Sit thou here in a good place; and say to the poor, Stand thou there, or sit here under my footstool:
⁴ Are ye not then partial in yourselves, and are become judges of evil thoughts?

In these three verses, God gives us an example to look at **to teach us a valuable lesson**. God gives us a picture of the church back then and today. As we look, we can see that not very much has changed. The picture that God is giving us is of two men coming into the church. The first is of **a rich man wearing very expensive clothing with a gold ring upon his hand**. It was the custom at that time to show off your riches because the belief was that the richer a person was, the closer he was to God.

Then, there was **a very poor man who came into the assembly**. His clothes were vile raiment. His description makes him little more than a beggar, if not a beggar. As we have already said, under Jewish belief, the more affluent or wealthy a person was, the more God had blessed and would continue to bless them. It is a shame that this attitude is still prevalent to a large degree in our churches today. **Clothes do not make the man**, is an old saying that seems to be forgotten by the church and by the Christian community.

The way people present themselves **does not make them a better or worse Christian**. There are two ways to look at this problem. A Christian does not need to flaunt their personal wealth. Doing so becomes a sin if they think others should look up to them because of their social position. According to scripture, we are to **be modest in our apparel**. At the same time, we are not to cast stones at those who are poor in material possessions. To be honest, often I have found that poor folks are the **happiest people of all**. To my amazement, many worldly people think that Christians are backward thinking, dowdy dressing, and fools for believing in God.

James chastises the church for their treatment of certain individuals. We are **not to prefer one person above another**. To do so goes against the teachings of the gospel. The rich and the poor **are to be treated the same**. The church also struggles with judging people by their past life and past deeds. If we are to be like our Lord Jesus, we must learn that **from the point of salvation, a person's past is not to be held against them**. If we hold their past against them, we might be the driving force that causes them to go back into the world and walk away from the Lord. True, a sinner must pay for his or her past crimes or sins even though they make things right with God, but our job as believers in the church of Jesus is to **accept their relationship with Christ as a valid reflection** of their newfound holiness through the redemptive blood Jesus shed on the cross for each of us.

A perfect example is as follows: There was a young woman in a certain town who sold her body to make her living. One night she attended a revival service in a full gospel church. The Lord gloriously **saved her and made her spiritually whole**. She became a **perfect model of what God can do in a heart and life that is sold out to Him**. About a year later, the pastor's son announced that this **young woman and he were going to get**

married. A large part of the church was against this marriage because she was not good enough for their pastor's son.

After all, she had been a woman of the night; she had sold her body to different men in her past. A few weeks later, **the pastor and his son stood before the congregation** on this matter. The pastor began by telling the people what he had been hearing. Then he reminded them of Mary Magdalene, who was a woman of the night until she met Jesus Christ. **After giving her heart to the Lord, she was a faithful follower of Jesus.** She was one of the faithful few who stood at the crucifixion of Jesus. He asked, "How many of you have stolen something in your past? How many have cursed, lied or done things in your past that you would be ashamed of if people knew about them? Nevertheless, Jesus **forgave you and made you clean** and whole."

Then the pastor's son began to speak. He told them that he **loved this girl and her past was not an issue**. They had talked about the way she used to be. Since Jesus had become the center of her life, **everything had changed.** She was **not who she used to be**. She was a **new creation, a new person.** He went on to say that **Jesus no longer held her past against her, and neither did he**. He was proud of her, they loved each other, and she was going to be his wife.

Although we hate to admit it, we must be careful not to show prejudice against others. We make snap judgements of others because of something we have been told, without finding out the truth for ourselves. If we listen to gossip, we will usually be misled and make the wrong decision. We cannot have respect of persons. We cannot **put one person over another**, for the Lord is not pleased with it. Know the **whole story, the whole truth, and let the Lord do the judging**, for He is the rightful judge.

By all rights, none of us is fit to make heaven our home.

However, because of the eternal love of our Saviour, **by His mercy and grace**, we have the opportunity to **make heaven our home**; not of anything we have done, but by the **amazing grace of God**.

Prejudice ruins lives, hurts feelings, and depresses people. This is why the scriptures teach the child of God **not to be prejudiced against others**.

The John Phillips Commentary Series states:

> Some years ago, I met a woman who liked to put this kind of behavior to the test. She would select a fashionable church and put on old, ill-fitting clothes, shabby shoes, and a dowdy hat. She would arrange her hair in an unsightly bun and present herself at the church. Her main interest was in finding out what kind of treatment she would receive at the door, either upon arrival or at the end of the service. Usually, little or no attention was paid to her at all. No one cared if she came or went. Usually, she received a perfunctory handshake at the door; the preacher's eyes being busy elsewhere.
>
> The next Sunday, she would present herself at the same church in a different guise, with styled hair, and wearing an expensive suit with a mink fur stole and expensive jewelry. On the way out, the pastor would be effusive.
>
> "We're so glad to have you with us. This must be your first visit. We do hope you'll come back. What is your name?"

She would look at him. "Oh, no, this is not my first visit. I was here last Sunday. As a matter of fact, you shook hands with me at the door then too."

"Surely not!"

"Oh yes. But, you see, last Sunday I dressed in old clothes, and you really didn't see me at all. You said a perfunctory, 'Good morning.' Then you hurried on to the lady behind me, who was much more stylishly dressed than I was. And, no, I shall not be back."

This kind of prejudice exists every day throughout this country. It is not limited to one denomination. It exists in all denominations where people have closed minds and preconceived ideas. We need to **pray until we are like Jesus**.

To be like Jesus,
To be like Jesus,
All I ask, is to be like Him,
All through life's journey
From earth to glory
All I ask is to be like Him.

In verse four, the judgement falls. How do we judge a person spirituality? Do we judge by their outward appearance, by the way they dress? We know that the scriptures teach that **Christians are to be modest in their apparel**. I believe that mature Christians should **dress as becomes holiness**. Yet I also know that Christians are in all stages of spiritual growth in becoming mature. Therefore, there is **no gage with which to**

judge everyone. All we can do is see **what kind of spiritual fruit they produce**.

As an example, what about the primitive people, some of whom go about half-naked? God is well able to save them; and after salvation, what then? From all reports I have read, they begin to **change as God deals with their hearts**. Would our modern churches accept their ways of dress? Probably not. However, **as long as God accepts them, that is all that counts**.

People today would not accept some of the things that went on in the church when I was growing up. Just as some of the things happening in the church today would not have been permitted in the 1940s, 50s, 60s or even the 1970s. Maybe this example was not such a good example, because many of the people who profess to being Christians today see nothing wrong with going half-naked in public, and the church accepts it without a word. This brings us to ask, what about Jesus? **Would the church world of today accept Jesus into their midst?** Probably not. Jesus, in His day, was **considered a religious rebel by the priesthood** and organized church leaders.

His teaching and preaching **did not fit into their religious traditions** and so He was rejected and despised. Jesus grew to manhood in the town of Nazareth, a town that was thought very poorly of. Jesus in this life was like most people, a poor man. He was not a handsome man. In fact, he was very plain and ordinary to look at. He dressed like the average poor man. In the book of Isaiah, we are told that *"he hath no form nor comeliness, and when we shall see him, there is no beauty that we should desire him."*

Isaiah 53:2-3

2 For he shall grow up before him as a tender plant, and

as a root out of a dry ground: he hath no form nor comeliness; and when we shall see him, there is no beauty that we should desire him.

³ He is despised and rejected of men; a man of sorrows, and acquainted with grief: and we hid as it were our faces from him; he was despised, and we esteemed him not.

However, **in the Father's house, Jesus is clothed with the righteousness, glory, and honor** due His station, because He is the **only begotten Son of God**. Moreover, He is our Saviour, our Redeemer, and our Soon Coming King. **To judge solely by the outward appearance is wrong.** We are not to have respect of people, because we are not to show partiality. Jesus made no distinction **between the rich and the poor**. What Jesus was concerned with was the soul, and **that is what is to be our primary concern**. Reach the soul first and address the other concerns second.

James 2:5-7

⁵ Hearken, my beloved brethren, Hath not God chosen the poor of this world rich in faith, and heirs of the kingdom which he hath promised to them that love him?
⁶ But ye have despised the poor. Do not rich men oppress you, and draw you before the judgment seats?
⁷ Do not they blaspheme that worthy name by the which ye are called?

James reinforces verse four in verse five. He begins verse five with a warning to **listen to what he has to say**. As we study this scripture, we see that **God choses the poor most of the time**

because they are rich in faith. The reason why is because they cannot rely on riches or social status because they have none. They must rely upon themselves or **put their faith in God**. James goes on to say that the heirs of the kingdom are those who **love God and have faith in Him**.

This world is getting worse and worse. It does not believe in God, only in itself. This world's trust is anchored in riches and possessions. The teaching of a God-created world is shunned in favor of evolution. The world teaches that man's only god is himself. He is what he is because of his own doings. God had nothing to do with his progress. It is a shame that man, it seems, has not learned to have faith in anything but himself. The world says to prove to them that there is a God. However, we as Christians need to state, "I know that there is a God. You prove to me that there is not." The scriptures teach us that **the fear of the Lord is the beginning of wisdom**.

Psalm 111:10

> *The fear of the LORD is the beginning of wisdom: a good understanding have all they that do his commandments: his praise endureth for ever.*

Proverbs 1:7

> *The fear of the LORD is the beginning of knowledge: but fools despise wisdom and instruction.*

With all of mankind's knowledge and all of his abilities; he is spiritually further in the dark than he has ever been. He has closed his heart to everything that is of God, not wanting to retain

God in any aspect of his life. Our public school systems do not teach even the possibility of God creating this world and all that is in it. The world would rather believe that life began in a primordial soup; that this life form crawled out of that primordial soup and changed by the process of evolution over billions of years to become what we now call the human race. However, the fact is that **God did create this world and all that is in it**. To the Christian, God gives us the assurance that **He is real and that we are the product of His hands** beginning with Adam and Eve in the garden, all the way down to us today.

To me, it is much easier to believe that **God made everything than that everything just came together and developed** into what we see around us. If people would only look, they would see a **God-created uniformity in all things**. The Christian people are accused of having vivid imaginations. Truthfully, who has the greater imagination?

Evolution is a theory; it is not a proven fact. However, as Carl Marx has said: "If you tell a lie long enough it becomes the truth." We are not the result of billions of years of evolutionary trial and errors. I do not know about you. My ancestors did not swing from a tree. Sometimes, I think that because of the way mankind has degenerated, people ought to apologize to the monkeys for claiming them as our ancestors. Some forty years ago, I ran across a poem that I would like for you to read.

The Three Monkeys

Three monkeys sat in a coconut tree
Discussing things as they're said to be.
Said one to the others, "Now listen you two
There's a certain rumor that can't be true,

That humans descended from our noble race.
The very ideal is a shocking disgrace.
Never did a monkey desert his wife,
Starved her babies and ruined her life.
And you've never known a mother monk
To leave her babies with others to bunk,
Or pass them on from one to another.
Till they scarcely know who is their mother.
And another thing you'll never see
A monk build a fence round a coconut tree.
And let the coconuts all go to waste.
Forbidding any other monks to taste.
Why, if I put a fence around a tree,
Starvation will force you to steal from me.
Here's another thing a monk won't do:
Go out at night and get on a stew,
Making whoopee with a gun or a knife,
And take some other monkey's life.
Yes, man descended, the ornery cuss,
But brother, he didn't descend from us."

                                    Author Unknown

In some ways, monkeys may be more civilized than man. Man is the only creature that hurts, maims and kills for the sheer pleasure they derive from it. No matter how smart man gets, he **cannot get away from himself**. When it comes to the matters of the spiritual, man has fallen way short; man only trusts in himself and what he possesses, **none of which impresses God**. Neither will it help his status when he stands before God. Jesus spoke about the **rich people of this world in the book of Matthew**.

Matthew 19:23-24

23 Then said Jesus unto his disciples, Verily I say unto you, That a rich man shall hardly enter into the kingdom of heaven.
24 And again I say unto you, It is easier for a camel to go through the eye of a needle, than for a rich man to enter into the kingdom of God.

Barnes' Notes on the New Testament says:

"Though poor in this world's goods, they are rich in a higher and more important sense. They have faith in God their Saviour; and in this world of trial and of sin, that is a more valuable possession than piles of hoarded silver or gold. A man who has that is sure that he will have all that is truly needful for him in this world and the next; a man who has it not, though he may have the wealth of Croesus, will be utterly without resources in respect to the great wants of his existence."

The poor who are **rich in faith are going to inherit the kingdom of heaven**. So has our God promised and so shall it be. We may be poor in this world's goods; however, we are **rich in the blessings of our Lord**. The rich young ruler who came to Jesus went away sorrowful because he had great possessions.

Luke 18:18-25

18 And a certain ruler asked him, saying, Good Master,

what shall I do to inherit eternal life?

19 And Jesus said unto him, Why callest thou me good? none is good, save one, that is, God.

20 Thou knowest the commandments, Do not commit adultery, Do not kill, Do not steal, Do not bear false witness, Honour thy father and thy mother.

21 And he said, All these have I kept from my youth up.

22 Now when Jesus heard these things, he said unto him, Yet lackest thou one thing: sell all that thou hast, and distribute unto the poor, and thou shalt have treasure in heaven: and come, follow me.

23 And when he heard this, he was very sorrowful: for he was very rich.

24 And when Jesus saw that he was very sorrowful, he said, How hardly shall they that have riches enter into the kingdom of God!

25 For it is easier for a camel to go through a needle's eye, than for a rich man to enter into the kingdom of God.

In today's world, man has become very arrogant where God is concerned. The general rule among the elite is that there is no God. It seems that the more highly educated people are, the less they believe in Jesus Christ the Son of God. Many, in their arrogance, have concluded that they are their own god. Without any help, the human race has pulled itself up by its own bootstraps and decided that it does not need the help of God. Is man partial? Is he prejudiced? Yes! He certainly is. The rich and socially prominent feel that they are better than the poor. They feel that those under them owe them something.

However, in the very near future, **our Saviour is coming to get us**. We will **enter that heavenly kingdom**, just as our God has promised. The only ones who are going in the rapture of the saints are those **who are rich in faith before God**. After we are gone, some will wake up to what has happened. How many, I cannot say; however, not great multitudes as some have proclaimed.

James goes on to say to the more affluent in the church: "You have despised the poor. Why, because they have less than you? They don't dress as well as you? Are not you yourselves despised by those who have more than you and still you have no compassion on those with less than you?" Why, when people are despised and rejected, do they look for others to whom they can do the same thing?

Where is Christian love and compassion? When the world mocks us, despises us, rejects us, and takes our Lord's name in vain, some through ignorance and some through hate, our position is to **pray for them that God will somewhere, somehow break them down** until they **accept Jesus as their loving Saviour**. Though we may weep in the night, joy comes in the morning.

Psalm 30:5

> *For his anger endureth but a moment; in his favour is life: weeping may endure for a night, but joy cometh in the morning.*

Paul in his writings to the Corinthian church speaks of "them which are called both Jews and Greeks." To these Christ is **the power of God and the wisdom of God**. Paul goes on to write about the Christian calling and how that not many wise men of this world and not many noble men are called.

1 Corinthians 1:26-27

^{26} For ye see your calling, brethren, how that not many wise men after the flesh, not many mighty, not many noble, are called:
^{27} But God hath chosen the foolish things of the world to confound the wise; and God hath chosen the weak things of the world to confound the things which are mighty;

The only way to stay saved is to **keep our faith in God and pray**, and to **trust and believe**. We need to reflect upon God or think upon the things of God, His wisdom and righteousness, and His sanctification and His redeeming power so that **the God of heaven might receive glory and honor from us**, His children. Seeing that all these things have been given unto us, what manner of person ought we to be? We are to **show forth the love of Christ to everyone**, not being a respecter of persons, showing no partiality but treating all men equal. Not bringing shame upon the name of Christ, but instead **showing His love and mercy to all men everywhere**.

We may be poor in this world's goods; however, **we are a child of the King**. Being a Christian is the only life that I know where **there is an abiding peace**. We do not know what is going to happen tomorrow; however, we do know **who holds tomorrow**. Come life or death, **we are safe in the hands of God**. There may be those who hate us and misuse us, however, **we still have peace**. The enemy, old Satan, is doing all he can to destroy God's church.

The mood of the populace seems to be turning against God's people. Whatever happens, remember that the world has judged us as bigots because we refuse to accept their morals and standards. **Stand for Jesus and know that He stands beside us to give us everything we need to make heaven our eternal home.**

James 2:8-10

⁸ If ye fulfil the royal law according to the scripture, Thou shalt love thy neighbour as thyself, ye do well:
⁹ But if ye have respect to persons, ye commit sin, and are convinced of the law as transgressors.
¹⁰ For whosoever shall keep the whole law, and yet offend in one point, he is guilty of all.

James in this eighth verse speaks of the royal law. They that obey it do well. But what is this royal law? To find the answer we need to go back to the time when **God gave the law to Moses**. In Leviticus, God **gives the law to Moses to give to the people**. The Lord tells the people that **they shall love their neighbors as they love themselves**.

Leviticus 19:17-18

¹⁷ Thou shalt not hate thy brother in thine heart: thou shalt in any wise rebuke thy neighbour, and not suffer sin upon him.
¹⁸ Thou shalt not avenge, nor bear any grudge against the children of thy people, but thou shalt love thy neighbour as thyself: I am the LORD.

If we obey the law that Jesus brought forward into the New Testament, then we **do well and give glory and honor to our Lord**.

The Wiersbe Bible Commentary: NT tells us:

> Why is "love thy neighbor" called "the royal law"? For one thing, it was given by the King. God the Father gave it in the law, and God the Son reaffirmed it to His disciples (John 13:34), God the Spirit fills our hearts with God's love and expects us to share it with others (Rom. 5:5). True believers are "taught of God to love one another" (1 Thess. 4:9).
>
> But "love thy neighbor" is the royal law for a second reason: *it rules all the other laws.* "Love is the fulfilling of the law" (Rom. 13:10). There would be no need for the thousands of complex laws if each citizen truly loved his neighbors.
>
> But the main reason why this is the royal law is that obeying it makes you a king. Hatred makes a person a slave, but love sets us free from selfishness and enables us to reign like kings. Love enables us to obey the Word of God and treat people as God commands us to do. We obey His law, not out of fear, but out of love.

The love of God is the **basis for all that we do in our walk with God**. Our Christian love, our love for the things of God, **builds our faith to trust and believe**, when commonsense tells us it is no use hoping or expecting, and we should just give up. However, **love builds an expectation in our heart**. When we pray and ask of God, the Word tells us to **expect to receive and we shall receive**.

In the book of Acts, chapter three, there was a lame man

who was laid at the gate of the temple, the gate called Beautiful. This lame man saw Peter and John about to go into the temple and asked alms of them. The scripture tells us that **he expected to receive something of them**. Peter told the lame man that they did not have any money; however, **such as he had, he would give unto him**. He said, "In the name of Jesus Christ of Nazareth, rise up and walk." The man rose and **went into the temple praising God**.

Acts 3:1-8

[1] Now Peter and John went up together into the temple at the hour of prayer, being the ninth hour.

[2] And a certain man lame from his mother's womb was carried, whom they laid daily at the gate of the temple which is called Beautiful, to ask alms of them that entered into the temple;

[3] Who seeing Peter and John about to go into the temple asked an alms.

[4] And Peter, fastening his eyes upon him with John, said, Look on us.

[5] And he gave heed unto them, expecting to receive something of them.

[6] Then Peter said, Silver and gold have I none; but such as I have give I thee: In the name of Jesus Christ of Nazareth rise up and walk.

[7] And he took him by the right hand, and lifted him up: and immediately his feet and ankle bones received strength.

[8] And he leaping up stood, and walked, and entered with them into the temple, walking, and leaping, and praising God.

If Peter had respect of persons, this lame beggar would never have been healed. Respect of persons is a sin, and they who do such things have their eyes blinded by Satan. James called such people sinners against the law of God. A lawyer approached Jesus in an effort to tempt Him. Jesus asked the lawyer what the law said. The lawyer replied, "Thou shalt love the Lord thy God with all thy heart," and ended with, "and thy neighbor as thyself." Jesus answered him, "This is right, do this, and you will live."

Luke 10:25-28

> *[25] And, behold, a certain lawyer stood up, and tempted him, saying, Master, what shall I do to inherit eternal life?*
> *[26] He said unto him, What is written in the law? how readest thou?*
> *[27] And he answering said, Thou shalt love the Lord thy God with all thy heart, and with all thy soul, and with all thy strength, and with all thy mind; and thy neighbour as thyself.*
> *[28] And he said unto him, Thou hast answered right: this do, and thou shalt live.*

It is imperative that we **love everyone, that we show no partiality**. Yet being a Christian does not mean that we will like everyone we meet. There might be things about a person that we do not like. We may not like how they act or talk; we may not like their lifestyle. Yet, we must have a **genuine love for their soul and treat them the way** Jesus would treat them.

James was **well schooled in the Law of Moses**. James was a Jew, brought up in Judaism. He became a Christian but still **held to his Jewish upbringing as closely as possible**. James was well respected by almost everyone, save the Jewish priesthood who sought to do away with him. **James understood and practiced the royal law.**

Barnes' Notes on the New Testament clarifies this for us:

> *If we fulfil the royal law.* That is, the law which he immediately mentions requiring us to love our neighbour as ourselves. It is called a *'royal* law' or *kingly* law, on account of its excellence or nobleness: not because it is ordained by God *as a king*, but because it has some such prominence and importance among other laws as a king has among other men; that is, it is majestic, noble, worthy of veneration. It is a law which ought to govern and direct us in all our intercourse with men - as a king rules his subjects.

We are to consider **everyone as our neighbor**. We are not to look down on or judge anyone because of their race, color, or creed. To prejudge a person keeps us from really finding out what they are like. You may find out that **you really like them**, that they are **a wonderful person, a good friend**.

When we show respect of a person, we are breaking the law of God. Today, we have what we call **the golden rule**. It says to **treat others as you would have them to treat you**. It does not say to love others as we love ourselves. It is the world's adaptation of loving one another, but **without any love being present**. The world tries to change God's law to bring it down to their level. For example, the Ten Commandments of God are now thought of by the world as the ten suggestions of God. It is up to us to obey them. Or not. How far have we fallen?

In verse nine, James continues by saying that if you have respect of persons, then you have committed sin in the sight of Almighty God. We have already talked about prejudice. Prejudice causes hatred among people and never brings about any good. In growing up where I did, I was never around people ethnically different from me. Nothing that I heard about the other races was good. However, when I graduated high school and went to work, I learned that **all races have good people and a few bad ones**. I made **good friends from other ethnic groups**. That old saying is very true, **if you want friends you must show yourself friendly**.

In verse ten, James makes a very important statement. You can keep the whole law, yet if a person offends in one point, then he is guilty of all. The scripture tells us that a little leaven leaveneth the whole lump. In other words, if you are guilty of the least, then you are guilty of the whole. For example, a little white lie is just as bad as any other sin, and the results are the same in the sight of God.

1 Corinthians 5:6-7

6 Your glorying is not good. Know ye not that a little leaven leaveneth the whole lump?
7 Purge out therefore the old leaven, that ye may be a new lump, as ye are unleavened. For even Christ our passover is sacrificed for us:

Galatians 5:9

A little leaven leaveneth the whole lump.

It is time that the church begins to stress the true Word of God and what it says. **Now is no time for us to dilute the Word of God.** It has already been diluted enough. Believe the **truth of what God's Word says,** not what the world says.

James 2:11-13

11 For he that said, Do not commit adultery, said also, Do not kill. Now if thou commit no adultery, yet if thou kill, thou art become a transgressor of the law.
12 So speak ye, and so do, as they that shall be judged by the law of liberty.
13 For he shall have judgment without mercy, that hath shewed no mercy; and mercy rejoiceth against judgment.

In the eleventh verse, James gives us an example of what he is saying in the previous verses. James tells us the **Lord gave us the law.** Thou shalt not **commit adultery, and do not kill.** You may not have committed adultery; however, if you have killed someone, you have become a transgressor of the law. In other words, you have become a sinner in the sight of God. It is human nature to always look for a loophole to justify one's self for doing something wrong.

It is a fact that each of us has our own weak spots, something that tempts us more than anything else does. Like all of us, there are things that do not tempt us at all. Then there are those things that affect us sorely. All men and women are tempted to sin. Samson's downfall was one particular woman. Anger caused Moses to be unable to enter the Promised Land. Solomon's greatest temptation was women. He had seven hundred wives and three hundred concubines. David committed adultery with

110

Bathsheba, then had her husband killed so that he could marry her.

The devil tempts all of us daily. However, remember that it is **not a sin when the devil tempts us**. The sin comes when we yield to the temptation put before us. For some unknown reason that I have yet to find, people have come to believe that they have committed a sin when they are tempted by the devil. However, this is not scriptural, because we have a choice. We can commit the sin, or we can **refuse the temptation and tell Satan to get behind us**, that we want nothing to do with it. Never forget that **we are the ones who make the choice**. Whether we commit sin or not is up to us.

There is a false doctrine in the world today. It says that after a person gives their heart to the Lord at salvation, if they continue to sin, they will not be judged for those sins. This belief is a falsehood. Any belief that teaches that a person who is saved can continue to sin and then will not be judged for those sins is foolish and unwise. They do not have an understanding of the Word of God.

Romans 6:1-2, 12-18

¹ What shall we say then? Shall we continue in sin, that grace may abound?
² God forbid. How shall we, that are dead to sin, live any longer therein?
¹² Let not sin therefore reign in your mortal body, that ye should obey it in the lusts thereof.
¹³ Neither yield ye your members as instruments of unrighteousness unto sin: but yield yourselves unto God, as those that are alive from the dead, and your members

as instruments of righteousness unto God.

[14] For sin shall not have dominion over you: for ye are not under the law, but under grace.

[15] What then? shall we sin, because we are not under the law, but under grace? God forbid.

[16] Know ye not, that to whom ye yield yourselves servants to obey, his servants ye are to whom ye obey; whether of sin unto death, or of obedience unto righteousness?

[17] But God be thanked, that ye were the servants of sin, but ye have obeyed from the heart that form of doctrine which was delivered you.

[18] Being then made free from sin, ye became the servants of righteousness.

The judgement of sinners when they stand before God will be a judgement without any mercy. All unforgiven sin will be judged. Every sin brings condemnation from God and must be forgiven. There is no such thing as "once you are saved you are always saved." Remember the statement that James said in verse ten. **If a man or woman keeps the whole law, yet offends in one point, they are guilty of all.**

This brings to mind an interesting talk I had with a man I worked with. We were talking about something he had said. He made the comment that he had told a little white lie. I asked him to tell me what a little white lie was. He told me that it was something he had said to keep from hurting someone's feelings. Being the person that I am, I asked him where in the Bible God says that it is all right to tell a lie. Lying is a sin, and the Word states that all liars will have their place in hell with all of the other sinners.

112

He tried to give me some lame excuse about it being all right because he was thinking about not hurting someone's feelings. I tried to explain that a lie is a lie. There are no little lies or big lies, no white lies or black lies. We may want there to be areas of gray; however, **God sees in black and white, in right and wrong**. A lie is a sin, big or small, black or white, according to God's Word. Whereupon my friend told me, "Well, you believe it your way, and I will believe it mine." **The Word is the Word, and like it or not, the Word of God will judge us.**

In this twelfth verse, James gives us some very important advice. We are to walk and talk each day **as if it were our last day to be alive**. Let no evil be found within you, knowing that one day we will answer for each and every unforgiven sin that might be within us. **God is merciful, seek His face, live according to His Word and all will be well.**

In this thirteenth verse, James speaks of God who will judge us, and if we have no mercy on others, then we will be judged without mercy. As we read what James is saying, we need to look at ourselves. We are **saved by grace through God's great mercy**. We are **free from the sin that condemned us**. We are **free from the harshness of the law**. We are **free to praise and give glory to our Redeemer**.

We have obtained mercy **through the blood of Jesus Christ our Saviour and Lord**. The act of mercy is the withholding of judgement. Throughout the Bible, we find episodes where mercy is given. Today, many times we associate **forgiveness with mercy**, and truly, **they are interwoven**. However, you can be shown mercy and still not be forgiven. When we stand before God, let us stand with no hatred or ill will toward anyone, but with **love for our God and His forgiving mercy**.

James 2:14-18

¹⁴ What doth it profit, my brethren, though a man say he hath faith, and have not works? can faith save him?
¹⁵ If a brother or sister be naked, and destitute of daily food,
¹⁶ And one of you say unto them, Depart in peace, be ye warmed and filled; notwithstanding ye give them not those things which are needful to the body; what doth it profit?
¹⁷ Even so faith, if it hath not works, is dead, being alone.
¹⁸ Yea, a man may say, Thou hast faith, and I have works: shew me thy faith without thy works, and I will shew thee my faith by my works.

In the fourteenth verse, James asks a question that is still debated today. **Is a person saved by grace or saved by works?** I believe that **faith is the key to living a Christ-like life**. We are saved by the **grace of God in Christ Jesus**. At salvation, we **begin our journey to heaven walking by faith**. James states in this verse, "What doth it profit, my brethren, though a man say he hath faith, and have not works: can faith save him?" We have heard it said that faith without works is dead. Can we then say that works without faith is dead, also?

Ephesians 2:8-10

⁸ For by grace are ye saved through faith; and that not of yourselves: it is the gift of God:
⁹ Not of works, lest any man should boast.
¹⁰ For we are his workmanship, created in Christ Jesus unto good works, which God hath before ordained that we

114

should walk in them.

James goes on to say that if a Christian man or woman sees someone who is in need and they do nothing to help them, then they have sinned in the sight of God. **We are not to wish them Godspeed if we have not done our best to meet their needs.** In the days of the early church, it was the church's responsibility to take care of the poor, the widows and orphans.

We know there are many who say they possess faith, but it is a dead faith, a faith in words only. Like many in our churches, they know how to talk the talk. However, they do not walk the walk. Too many churches today teach the same thing, as did the rabbinical law. Their primary emphasis is on works. Yes, we are **to do good deeds**. First, we are to **help our Christian family**, for this is the will of God. The scripture says if we see a brother or sister in need (talking about our Christian family), we are to **help them if possible**. Remember, as we do these good deeds to others, the Word teaches **that we do them to Jesus**.

In verses seventeen and eighteen, Jesus teaches us that **if we have faith only, without works, our faith is dead**. It gives no glory or honor to the Lord who called us to salvation. Paul, on the other hand, warns us against only having dead works. The Jews looked to doing good works to gain the approval of God and to be in His favor. Paul preached that **we live by faith, and our faith produces good works**.

Hebrews 6:1

Therefore leaving the principles of the doctrine of Christ, let us go on unto perfection; not laying again the foundation of repentance from dead works, and of faith

115

toward God,

Hebrews 9:14

How much more shall the blood of Christ, who through the eternal Spirit offered himself without spot to God, purge your conscience from dead works to serve the living God?

Then we look at the scriptures written in:

Ephesians 2:4-16

4 But God, who is rich in mercy, for his great love wherewith he loved us,
5 Even when we were dead in sins, hath quickened us together with Christ, (by grace ye are saved;)
6 And hath raised us up together, and made us sit together in heavenly places in Christ Jesus:
7 That in the ages to come he might shew the exceeding riches of his grace in his kindness toward us through Christ Jesus.
8 For by grace are ye saved through faith; and that not of yourselves: it is the gift of God:
9 Not of works, lest any man should boast.
10 For we are his workmanship, created in Christ Jesus unto good works, which God hath before ordained that we should walk in them.
11 Wherefore remember, that ye being in time past Gentiles in the flesh, who are called Uncircumcision by that which is called the Circumcision in the flesh made by hands;
12 That at that time ye were without Christ, being aliens

116

from the commonwealth of Israel, and strangers from the covenants of promise, having no hope, and without God in the world:

¹³ But now in Christ Jesus ye who sometimes were far off are made nigh by the blood of Christ.

¹⁴ For he is our peace, who hath made both one, and hath broken down the middle wall of partition between us;

¹⁵ Having abolished in his flesh the enmity, even the law of commandments contained in ordinances; for to make in himself of twain one new man, so making peace;

¹⁶ And that he might reconcile both unto God in one body by the cross, having slain the enmity thereby:

2 Timothy 1:9

Who hath saved us, and called us with an holy calling, not according to our works, but according to his own purpose and grace, which was given us in Christ Jesus before the world began,

Here we find that **we are saved by faith**. Our salvation as we walk in the newness of life in Christ Jesus **will produce good works**. If the church will **believe and stand by faith, we will be surprised by what God can and will do**. With a Christ-like spirit and a Godly love, we can **reach this lost and dying world for Jesus**.

God is looking for men and women who are willing to give of themselves, **regardless of what the cost may be**. I have known of people who have said, "Why, that is me. Count me in. I am ready to help." However, when the going got tough, they were soon ready to quit and go home. **Jesus was careful who He**

117

chose. All but Judas were men that Jesus knew would **stand the test to the very end**. Those men were men who were **dedicated to the calling Jesus placed upon them**.

Paul was the same kind of man as the disciples. He was a man **dedicated to the calling that Jesus placed upon him**. There was **no cost too great** to follow Jesus. This is what the Lord is looking for today, for those who are **willing to do what is necessary** to fulfill the Lord's calling. You can be that man or woman. Put your **trust and faith in Jesus** and say, "Yes Lord, here I am. Use me, Oh Lord."

We are to remind ourselves to be **used of God to further His labor**. Not just for our main area of service such as being a minister or missionary, song leader or janitor, teacher or altar worker; we are to ask Him to **use us in our daily life**. So remember to **ask Jesus what to do each day and then do it no matter how insignificant or demeaning** you think it is, and God will bless you.

James 2:19-20

> [19] *Thou believest that there is one God; thou doest well:*
> *the devils also believe, and tremble.*
> [20] *But wilt thou know, O vain man, that faith without works*
> *is dead?*

James is making a statement that most people seem to have forgotten. There is **only one God**. He is manifested in three persons who make up the Godhead: **God the Father, God the Son (Jesus Christ) and God the Holy Ghost**. We believe that the triune Godhead that we call the trinity exists, for according to scripture, **Jesus is the only begotten Son of God**. The Holy

Ghost is the **promised comforter sent to us by Jesus**.

We do not believe in polytheism (a belief in more than one God). Nor do we believe in pantheism (a belief that all the forces of the universe are God) as many people do. These people are misled into believing these doctrines by the tricks of Satan. James reinforces our belief in only one God by stating that the devils also believe and know that there is only one God, and they **tremble at the thought of what God is going to do to them** in the near future.

As Jesus walked upon this earth, He dealt with many demons or devils, all of whom knew who He was. They knew that Jesus was the **only begotten Son of God**. Remember in scripture where we are told that Jesus went into the country of the Gergesenes. There He met two men possessed of many devils. These devils **knew who Jesus was**, and they called Him the Son of God. Then they asked Jesus a question: "Art thou come hither to torment us before the time?" They knew that **their time was limited, and then would come judgement**.

Matthew 8:28-32

> *28 And when he was come to the other side into the country of the Gergesenes, there met him two possessed with devils, coming out of the tombs, exceeding fierce, so that no man might pass by that way.*
>
> *29 And, behold, they cried out, saying, What have we to do with thee, Jesus, thou Son of God? art thou come hither to torment us before the time?*
>
> *30 And there was a good way off from them an herd of many swine feeding.*
>
> *31 So the devils besought him, saying, If thou cast us out,*

119

suffer us to go away into the herd of swine.
³² And he said unto them, Go. And when they were come out, they went into the herd of swine: and, behold, the whole herd of swine ran violently down a steep place into the sea, and perished in the waters.

All of us will, on that judgement day, **stand before God and be judged according to our works**. James goes on to tell us again that **faith without works is dead**. What James is saying is that if we have faith, then we will **have good works because of Christ**, who lives within us. Again, if there are no good works, then our faith is dead. The question we must ask ourselves is **whether our faith is alive or dead**. If we want dynamic faith, a faith that we know will bring results, then we **must have a prayer life that is anchored** in Jesus Christ.

True faith in Jesus Christ **gives the believer power with God to the working of miracles**. Many people today have faith; however, their faith is a misguided faith. When people bow before idols, be they gods of stone, wood or gold, their faith is in vain. Idols have no life and cannot work on our behalf. The Lord God is the **only God who is alive and hears our prayers** and moves on our behalf. No matter how much faith a person may have, if it is not channeled into the **one and only true God, that faith is a counterfeit faith** and reaches no higher than the ceiling. True faith in Jesus **produces works of love and kindness**. It lifts the hearts of people everywhere.

The Wiersbe Bible Commentary: NT makes this clear:

Dynamic faith is based on God's Word, and it *involves the whole man*. Dead faith touches only

120

the intellect; demonic faith involves both the mind and the emotions; but dynamic faith involves the will. The whole person plays a part in true saving faith. The mind understands the truth; the heart desires the truth; and the will acts upon the truth. The men and women of faith named in Hebrews 11 were people of action: God spoke and they obeyed. Again, "Faith is not believing in spite of evidence; faith is obey in spite of consequence."

True saving faith *leads to action.* Dynamic faith is not intellectual contemplation or emotional consternation; it leads to obedience on the part of the will. And this obedience is not an isolated event: it continues throughout the whole life. It leads to works.

Ephesians 2:8-9

[8] For by grace are ye saved through faith; and that not of yourselves: it is the gift of God:
[9] Not of works, lest any man should boast.

We are **saved by grace through faith and not by works lest any should boast**. We all come to Jesus the same way, for in Christ Jesus there are no big "I's" and little "you's." We are all the same. We are **brothers and sisters in the family of God**.

James 2:21-24

[21] Was not Abraham our father justified by works, when he had offered Isaac his son upon the altar?

22 Seest thou how faith wrought with his works, and by works was faith made perfect?
23 And the scripture was fulfilled which saith, Abraham believed God, and it was imputed unto him for righteousness: and he was called the Friend of God.
24 Ye see then how that by works a man is justified, and not by faith only.

James, as we have already said, is still tied to Judaism and the belief that works open the kingdom of God. This is one reason why the Jewish people have such a hard time accepting salvation in Jesus Christ through grace, because they are taught that their salvation comes through works.

In verse twenty-one, James begins to give us another illustration. James brings up what the Word says about Abraham.

Hebrews 11:8-19

8 By faith Abraham, when he was called to go out into a place which he should after receive for an inheritance, obeyed; and he went out, not knowing whither he went.
9 By faith he sojourned in the land of promise, as in a strange country, dwelling in tabernacles with Isaac and Jacob, the heirs with him of the same promise:
10 For he looked for a city which hath foundations, whose builder and maker is God.
11 Through faith also Sara herself received strength to conceive seed, and was delivered of a child when she was past age, because she judged him faithful who had promised.
12 Therefore sprang there even of one, and him as good as

122

dead, so many as the stars of the sky in multitude, and as the sand which is by the sea shore innumerable.

13 These all died in faith, not having received the promises, but having seen them afar off, and were persuaded of them, and embraced them, and confessed that they were strangers and pilgrims on the earth.

14 For they that say such things declare plainly that they seek a country.

15 And truly, if they had been mindful of that country from whence they came out, they might have had opportunity to have returned.

16 But now they desire a better country, that is, an heavenly: wherefore God is not ashamed to be called their God: for he hath prepared for them a city.

17 By faith Abraham, when he was tried, offered up Isaac: and he that had received the promises offered up his only begotten son,

18 Of whom it was said, That in Isaac shall thy seed be called:

19 Accounting that God was able to raise him up, even from the dead; from whence also he received him in a figure.

We first find Abraham before God changed his name. Abram lived in Haran in the land of Ur of the Chaldees. There God spoke to Abram and told him to **leave his home and follow Him to a land** that God would show him. Abram packed up all he had and, with his wife, **left all that he knew to follow God**. Abram's wife was Sarai, his half-sister, and she was barren. After God spoke to Abram, his whole life was dedicated to serving God. **Abram believed God and walked with God.**

When Abram was ninety-nine years old, God appeared to him, and said, *"I am the Almighty God; walk before me and be thou perfect."* (Genesis 17:1) Then in the same chapter, verse five, God changes Abram's name to Abraham, and in verse fifteen, God changes Sarai's name to Sarah. Abraham and Sarah had their promised son in their old age.

Isaac was the child of promise. When Isaac was a young boy, God spoke to Abraham and told him to take Isaac, his only son, and sacrifice him on an altar to God. Abraham built an altar, put the wood on the altar and prepared to take Isaac's life, believing that **even if Isaac died, the Lord would restore him** back to life. Oh, the faith that Abraham had in God.

James states that Abraham's faith was **made perfect by works**. I believe in works; however, **works do not take the place of faith**. I can see what James is saying and what he means. Our faith is **made perfect by obedience**. God, in asking Abraham to offer up Isaac, was testing Abraham's obedience to Him. Works or not, **without obedience to God, it is impossible** to please God. Abraham had the kind of relationship that we all wish and hope to have with God. The scripture says in 1 Samuel 15:22: *"Behold, to obey is better than sacrifice."* Even today, people do not understand Christians **who put their trust in God**. You will find that many times we make things worse for ourselves when we do not give our problems to the Lord. There are too many people today who profess to be living a Christian life, but their heart is far from God.

Titus 1:15-16

[15] Unto the pure all things are pure: but unto them that are defiled and unbelieving is nothing pure; but even their

124

mind and conscience is defiled.
¹⁶ They profess that they know God; but in works they deny
him, being abominable, and disobedient, and unto every
good work reprobate.

In verse twenty-four, James is still speaking of how we are justified by works and not faith alone. He reminds me of a preacher that I know. He was telling me what he believed and why, and as I listened to what he said, I realized that **we believed the same thing**. He was just saying it a different way. We need to **listen to what people say**. It might **surprise you what you can learn**.

James 2:25-26

²⁵ Likewise also was not Rahab the harlot justified by
works, when she had received the messengers, and had
sent *them* out another way?
²⁶ For as the body without the spirit is dead, so faith
without works is dead also

The second illustration James gives is about Rahab the harlot, a woman who lived in Jericho. As the Hebrews were approaching Jericho, Joshua decided to **send two spies into the land around about the city of Jericho,** instructing them to go into the city and search it out. The spies were to **learn everything they could about the defenses** and the inhabitants of the place. The spies went into the city and **stayed in the house of Rahab** the harlot.

A report of the spies being seen was given to the King of Jericho. He sent word to Rahab to give up the spies. Rahab

instead hid them in her house, which was upon the wall. Rahab told the spies that the people of the city were afraid of the Hebrews. They had all heard how their God helped them to cross the Red Sea; how God had parted the waters for them to cross on dry ground; how God had helped the Hebrews to defeat the two kings of the Amorites; but that **she knew God was going to give them the land**.

The King's men began to search outside the city walls for the spies. All this time, they remained hidden by Rahab. She talked to the spies and asked them that **when they took Jericho, to spare her and her family**. They told her that if she kept her word about their escape, when they returned and took the city, **everyone in her house would be spared**. However, they must be in her house. If they were outside of the house, they would be killed. She agreed to their words. She put **her faith in their honesty with her**. After dark, because her house was built on the top of the wall, she let them down to the ground from a window in the side of her house.

When the spies returned to Joshua, they told him of the agreement they had made with Rahab. **God honored Rahab's faith, and she and her household were saved**. Rahab would become **part of the linage of King David and of Jesus Christ**.

God honors faith **regardless of who the person may be**. James goes on to tell us that a body without the spirit is dead. In addition, faith without works is dead. Rahab had faith and put her faith in the God of the Hebrews. **Rahab's faith, combined with her works, saved her household.**

Many people state that they believe in God; however, their lives show no sign of it. The main question is what kind of faith you have, and do you have works to go with it?

126

Chapter 2 Review Questions

1. What are the two main groups in the Christian movement and briefly what do they believe?

_____

_____

_____

2. Christians and the church needs to learn that in Christ Jesus we cannot have what in our lives?

_____

_____

3. What has caused more wars than any other thing?

_____

_____

_____

4. What is the most precious thing that a person possesses?

_____

_____

_____

5. We as a whole have a problem with judging people. Why?

_____

_____

_____

6. Why does having prejudice ruin lives?

_____

_____

_____

7. Why does God use the poor most of the time?

_____

_____

_____

8. The scriptures teach us that the fear of the Lord is:

_____

_____

9. What did Carl Marx believe? Give an example.

_____

_____

10. What are the more highly educated people less likely to do?

_____

_____

_____

11. What is the royal law?

_____

_____

_____

12. Is it possible to love a person and not like them?

_____

_____

13. What was Solomon's greatest downfall?

_____

_____

_____

14. How many women did Solomon have?

_____

_____

15. What was King David's sin?

_____

_____

_____

16. Is it sin when we are tempted by Satan?

_____

_____

17. What is polytheism?

_____

_____

18. What is pantheism?

_____

_____

19. What question did the demons ask Jesus in the country of the

Gergesenes?

_____

_____

_____

20. What was the kinship between Abraham and Sarah?

_____

_____

_____

21. Why did God save Rahab and her household?

_____

_____

_____

Chapter 3

James 3:1

My brethren, be not many masters, knowing that we shall receive the greater condemnation.

James begins this chapter by dealing with a problem that was common then and still prevails today. Too many people desired to be teachers of the Word, **even though they did not have the qualifications to be teachers.** In verse one, James tells them that a **few teachers who are qualified is much better than many teachers who are unqualified.**

The people desired to be **instructors of God's Word rather than those receiving instruction.** I know that those whom the Lord calls, He qualifies, and that he can bring all things to our remembrance. Yet, you cannot remember something that you never learned. There must be some knowledge, some teaching received before a person can teach others. **It took Jesus three and one-half years to get the disciples qualified to start His church.** An unqualified teacher then and today is a danger to the true gospel of Jesus Christ. **Without a working knowledge of the scriptures, you cannot teach others.**

Today, we have **Bibles to read**. We have **Sunday school material** to follow a lesson plan. We have all manner of **research materials, some good and some not so good**. In James' day, in the early church, they had no such material. There was no Bible. There were no Bible colleges or schools. Biblical knowledge was handed down in two ways, by **word of mouth or a letter from one of the apostles**. It was very important to sit under a good teacher like Paul or one of the other apostles. This is why the New Testament is so important to us today. It is the **written Word of God**.

Christians in James' day, the ones he was writing to, had trouble watching what they were saying. Remember in James 1:19, the Word says to be *"swift to hear, slow to speak, slow to wrath."* Wise Christians should **learn to bridle their tongues**. The power of words is great and can be used for much good or great evil. Words are one of the few things that once said can never be taken back. We can ask for forgiveness for what we said; however, the words will be forever out there. Man is the only creature that with words can **lift up a person's esteem to great heights** or break someone's heart.

The Wiersbe Bible Commentary: NT reveals:

> In order to impress on us the importance of controlled speech, and the great consequences of our words, James gave us six pictures of the tongue: the bit, the rudder, fire, a poisonous animal, a fountain, and a fig tree. You can put these six pictures into three meaningful classifications that reveal the three powers of the tongue.

James wants us to see **the grave responsibility and accountability that we put ourselves in** when we must decide between one of two things: **what the self wants or what God desires**. I have heard many ministers, God-called to preach, say that at least once every week they want to quit preaching and give up the ministry. However, they do not give up because **they are God-called to preach His Word**.

Sadly, today many people know just enough to make them dangerous to their fellow brothers and sisters in the Lord. There are times when a little bit of knowledge is a dangerous thing, if we are not very careful. It is like changing out a light fixture. You go and buy a new fixture because the old one does not work. You get your ladder out and take down the old fixture. Everything is going well. You start wiring in the new fixture and someone comes along and flips on the light switch. The light does not light up, but you do, because you forgot to turn off the breaker. We must be very careful in everything we do.

Then and now people are the same. It is great to **have a zeal to do something** for the Lord. However, we must remember that before we can be effective, we must **know what we are doing**. It is great to **witness for the Lord, to tell people of what Jesus has done for you** and how He has transformed your life. However, it is another thing to try to teach God's Word when you do not know it yourself.

People in this type of situation, when confronted with something that they do not know, often try to make up something on the spur of the moment, something that sounds good to them. They do not want to admit that they do not know. I have made it a policy to tell people, "Well, I don't know, but I will find out for you." We must **always be honest**.

I have heard people say that Paul was called on the spur of

the moment. Yes, he was. However, Paul was a Pharisee and **highly educated in religious law**, and after Paul got back his sight, he went **into the desert for three years**, where I am sure the Lord schooled Paul in the gospel message. **Jesus taught the disciples for three years before He went back to heaven.**

Another very sobering thing is this. We, who are called to be ministers and teachers, are **accountable to the Lord for every soul that sits before us** and hears what we have to say. **As long as we preach the truth of God's Word, we are blameless before God.** However, if we preach or teach anything that is untrue and a soul misses heaven because of it, God holds us accountable for that lost soul. We must know the truth because it is the **only thing that will set men and women free**.

John 8:31-32

> [31] *Then said Jesus to those Jews which believed on him, If ye continue in my word, then are ye my disciples indeed;*
> [32] *And ye shall know the truth, and the truth shall make you free.*

Romans 8:2

> *For the law of the Spirit of life in Christ Jesus hath made me free from the law of sin and death.*

Now, as in the days of Paul, James, Peter and John, people do not realize the condemnation that can fall upon them if they preach and teach anything that is untrue. As ministers, we must stop to **consider our responsibility before God**.

Barnes' Notes on the New Testament tells us:

> *Knowing that we shall receive the greater condemnation*, Or rather, *a severer judgment*; that is, we shall have a severer trial, and give a stricter account. The word here used does not necessarily mean *condemnation*, but *judgment, trial, account*; and the consideration which the apostle suggests is not that those who were public teachers would be *condemned*, but that there would be a much more solemn account to be rendered by them than by other men, and that they ought duly to reflect on this in seeking the office of the ministry. He would carry them in anticipation before the judgment-seat, and have them determine the question of entering the ministry there. No better "stand-point" can be taken in making up the mind in regard to this work; and if that had been the position assumed in order to estimate the work, and to make up the mind in regard to the choice of this profession, many a one who has sought the office would have been deterred from it;

There is an old saying that a man should **look before he leaps and think before he speaks**. If we did this, there would be less trouble in the world today. With good friends, a person can joke and cutup. However, there are **certain subjects which should be left alone**. Never make jokes about a person's family, their religion, or their politics. As we say, "them are fighting words."

James 3:2

For in many things we offend all. If any man offend not in word, the same is a perfect man, and able also to bridle the whole body.

James begins by admitting that we **are all human and make mistakes**. Moreover, if we are not careful, we can offend those around us, and God forbid, sometimes we **never know we have offended them**. It is hard to keep ourselves in check sometimes. If we are not careful, we can allow ourselves to get into the flesh and **both offend and be offended**. I like what *Barnes' Notes* has to say.

Barnes' Notes on the New Testament says:

> The word here rendered *offend*, means to stumble, to fall; then to err, to fail in duty; and the meaning here is, that all were liable to commit error, and that this consideration should induce men to be cautious in seeking an office where an error would be likely to do so much injury. The particular thing, doubtless, which the apostle had in his eye, was the peculiar liability to commit error, or to do wrong with the tongue. Of course, this liability is very great in an office where the *very business* is public speaking. If anywhere the improper use of the tongue will do mischief, it is in the office of a religious teacher; and to show the danger of this, and the importance of caution in seeking that office, the apostle proceeds to show

what mischief the *tongue* is capable of effecting.

James in the next part of this verse says that a person who does not offend in word, the same is **a perfect man or woman who is able to bridle their whole body**. The hardest part of the body to control is one of the smallest parts, and **that part is the tongue**. It is the unruliest member of our bodies. We read in Psalms where King David said, "*I will take heed to my ways that I sin not with my tongue.*" Then, in Proverbs, Solomon wrote, "*Whoso keepth his mouth and his tongue keepth his soul from trouble.*"

Psalm 39:1

> *I said, I will take heed to my ways, that I sin not with my tongue: I will keep my mouth with a bridle, while the wicked is before me.*

Proverbs 21:23

> *Whoso keepeth his mouth and his tongue keepeth his soul from troubles.*

More people are offended by what is said to them and about them than any other thing. If we will follow what King David and King Solomon had to say, it will **keep us out of trouble and misfortune**. So, pray that you **offend no one**.

Sometimes we can offend and never know about it. This happened to me in the first church that we pastored. We were in the process of having a Sunday school campaign to see who could get **the most people to come to Sunday school**. This went for a period of six weeks. The prize was **a nice study Bible**. There were a man and his wife who were working very hard to win this Bible. Each **invited people to Sunday school**, and they **came on the same Sunday**. Here is where I made my mistake.

I asked them if they wanted to be listed separately or together. They said that it did not matter; **however, it did**. I listed them together, and I asked them whose name they wanted to be under, his or hers. I was again told that it did not matter; **however, it did**. I listed the guests under the wife's name, and **she won the Bible**. I could tell her husband was angry at me, although he never said anything about it.

They later left the church. This brother would not have anything to do with me. Years later, I discovered what the problem was. **I had awarded his wife that Bible and not him.** My wife and I bought a very nice study Bible, and a few days later, when I saw him at his sister's house, I apologized to him and told him that **I hadn't meant to hurt him**. If he had told me, we could have worked this out a long time ago. I presented him the Bible and apologized again. **From that time on, we were on good terms.**

My friends, sometimes we may **hurt someone's feelings and never know about it**. If we do not know, then we cannot do anything. If you are like me, we are not mind readers. There is nothing we can do about it **if God does not reveal it to us**, because we do not know about it. Therefore, **when we know we have offended someone, we are to do what Christ would do**. Go to them and apologize. If they forgive you, that is good. If not, then **you are not at fault**. You are blameless. **You have done what is right before God.**

We must pray and seek God for the **ability to control our tongue**. The tongue is the unruliest member of our bodies. He that can bridle the tongue does well. If you can bridle your tongue, then you have **complete control of yourself**, and scripture states that you are a **perfect individual before God**.

James 3:3-4

³ Behold, we put bits in the horses' mouths, that they may obey us; and we turn about their whole body.
⁴ Behold also the ships, which though they be so great, and are driven of fierce winds, yet are they turned about with a very small helm, whithersoever the governor listeth.

In verse three, James gives us an illustration. This verse gives us a look at **how we put bits in the mouths of horses to control them**. In nature, most animals are wild and hard to control. The horse is no exception. Its nature is **not to let man ride upon its back**. We have all seen pictures of horses being broken to ride. How, when the cowboy climbs up into the saddle, the horse fights to unseat the cowboy; it jumps and rears up, and it snorts and screams wildly.

If the cowboy does not give up, he **gains control over the animal**. The horse gives up, and **its spirit is broken**. Then the training begins, and the **horse learns to answer to the bit**. These bits are very uncomfortable to the horse until it learns to obey. Once it learns to obey the commands of the rider, it takes **just a small movement on the reins** for it to know what the rider wants. As the horse becomes sensitive to the reins, **so must we become sensitive to the moving of the spirit of the Lord**.

This, for some, is not easy; however, we **all learn by trial and error**. I can see where it is better some of the time to **be in error in trying to do something** for the Lord, than to **never do**

anything for God. As the Lord speaks to us, we **learn His voice**. In learning His voice, we find a **much closer relationship with Him**. A much better life lies ahead in serving Jesus Christ. It is wonderful when the Lord speaks to us, and no, we are not a mental case, as the world believes. We are **anchored to the rock**, we are **walking the right path** and **heaven is our home**.

In the fourth verse, James gives us another illustration that involves the **steering of a ship upon the sea**. Whether the ship is small or a giant cargo vessel, the **whole of it is steered by a rudder**. In James's day, ships were powered by oars or by the winds. No matter how they are powered, all are **steered by the turning of a rudder**. The rudder is small compared to the size of the ship. Though small, the rudder has the power to **turn the ship in any direction** the captain desires to go. Without the rudder, the ship would be **at the mercy of the winds, floundering help-lessly**.

The Bismarck was one of the two largest battleships built by Germany in World War II. At the time, the Bismarck was the largest battleship afloat. It had the largest guns and the thickest armor of any ship. When the British Navy attacked the Bismarck, the main reason the Bismarck sunk that day was a torpedo plane dropping a torpedo **that struck and damaged the rudder**. This caused the Bismarck to be locked into a twelve-degree turn to port. All the doomed ship could do was to turn in a large circle. **Not able to escape the British, the Bismarck was sunk.**

The mightiest battleship in the world at that time was defeated because of **her rudder being damaged and unable to turn** the ship as her captain desired. Every one of us has our Achilles heel. An Achilles heel is a **weakness despite our overall strength**, which can lead to a downfall; while of mythological origin, it refers to a **physical vulnerability**. Vulnerabilities in our spiritual lives can **also lead to a downfall**. We must guard ourselves against Satan's attacks.

The sinner is like a **ship with a broken rudder**. Without a good rudder, there is no way to steer your life **in the right direction**. Jesus, our Lord and Master, is the Christian's spiritual rudder steering us in the right direction. Jesus steers us into the **paths of righteousness that we may be a shining light in the darkness of this world**.

The Wiersbe Bible Commentary: NT helps explain:

> This means that both the bit and the rudder must be under the control of a strong hand. The expert horseman keeps the mighty power of his steed under control, and the experienced pilot courageously steers the ship through the storm. When Jesus Christ controls the tongue, then we need not fear saying the wrong things – or even saying the right things in a wrong way! "Death and life are in the power of the tongue," warned Solomon (Prov. 18:21). No wonder David prayed, "Set a watch, O Lord, before my mouth; keep the door of my lips. Incline not my heart to any evil thing" (Ps. 141:34), David knew that the heart is the key to right speech. "Out of the abundance of the heart the mouth speaketh" (Matt. 12:34). When Jesus Christ is the Lord of the heart, then He is Lord of the lips too.
>
> The bit and rudder have the power to direct, which means *they affect the lives of others*. A runaway horse or a shipwreck could mean injury or

death to pedestrians or passengers. The words we speak affect the lives of others. A judge says, "Guilty!" or "Not Guilty!" and those words affect the destiny of the prisoner, his family, and his friends.

Never underestimate the power of the words you speak. You have the power to **change lives forever**. It can be for the good or it can be for the bad. Once said, words can never be taken back, so guard what you say. Never speak rashly and **always think before you speak**, for souls may weigh in the balance. The words you speak may **lead someone to Jesus Christ** or turn him or her away from God forever.

Remember, we must **guard against the small foxes that desire to spoil the vine**.

Song of Solomon 2:15

Take us the foxes, the little foxes, that spoil the vines: for our vines have tender grapes.

Solomon, the **wisest man that ever lived**, knew the pitfalls of the enemy because he fell himself. In our lives, many times we will stumble and fall mostly because we are not on guard. Hold to God's unchanging hand and **take nothing for granted**. Be **wise as serpents and harmless as doves**.

James 3:5-6

[5] Even so the tongue is a little member, and boasteth great things. Behold, how great a matter a little fire kindleth!

*⁶ And the tongue is a fire, a world of iniquity: so is the
tongue among our members, that it defileth the whole
body, and setteth on fire the course of nature; and it is set
on fire of hell.*

James again speaks of the tongue being a little member,
yet with the tongue **great boasts are made**. Things are said, some
to the good and some to the bad. We must continually be **on our
guard against the enemy**, old Satan, and those who are around
us. However, often we are our own worst enemy. I have said
many times the devil would not have so much to throw at us if we
did not give it to him. The devil is not God, and he does not know
our inner thoughts, the thoughts of our heart. He only knows what
we let him know, so **keep your thoughts to yourself and you
will have a lot less trouble**.

There is an old story my pastor would tell sometimes
about a group of ladies that got together one time, and they
decided they would tell each other their hidden secrets.

One lady confessed that at times when she was alone, she
would drink and sometimes get drunk. One of the other ladies
confessed that she stole things. Oh, not anything large or costly,
but she would, given the opportunity, take something small and
inexpensive. Another lady said, "Well, I guess I can tell you, since
we are telling each other our secrets, that I am a compulsive liar. I
tell all kinds of lies, mostly little ones, although I never intend to
hurt anyone." Another lady bowed her head and turned a medium
shade of red before she spoke. Then she confessed to having an
affair with one of her neighbors down the street. She did not mean
for it to happen, it just did. Her husband was working so much,
and she got lonely and started talking to her neighbor, and before

long, they were in an affair.

Then only one lady was left, and they all looked at her with anticipation as to what she would say. Then she confessed that she was the world's worst gossip, and that she spread everything she heard; and now she could hardly wait till she got home so she could **tell everybody she knew what she had just learned**.

Too many times, we give the enemy everything he needs to make our lives miserable. A small member of the body, the tongue **can speak life**, or it can speak death. Oh, the power that the tongue holds.

Peter preached on the day of Pentecost, and some **three thousand repented of their sins and accepted Jesus Christ** as their Saviour because the tongue **spoke the words of life**. Ministers, missionaries and Bible teachers have **led millions to Christ** with words spoken by the tongue. Yet, millions have died around the world because of words spoken in anger and malice. Every war that has been fought was fought because of angry words spoken in hatred and malice. The tongue is a fire, and too many times it kindles great things. James writes in verse six that the tongue is a world of iniquity, and if allowed to follow the course of nature, it causes all sorts of problems. He also goes on to say that it is set on fire by the pits of hell.

Spoken lies sent Jesus to the cross. By the tongue, the crowd called for Jesus to be crucified. The church world and church leaders of the Middle Ages caused millions to be killed. The Catholic Church caused millions of Christians to be put to death because they refused to believe the Catholic doctrine. The Pope again caused millions to die by calling for a holy war to retake the Holy Land. The truth being known, the Roman Catholic

Church is responsible for the death of multiplied millions of people, Christians and non-Christians. **If the church lived by and preached the gospel, the world would be a different place today**, this I truly believe.

James 3:7-10

[7] For every kind of beasts, and of birds, and of serpents, and of things in the sea, is tamed, and hath been tamed of mankind:
[8] But the tongue can no man tame; it is an unruly evil, full of deadly poison.
[9] Therewith bless we God, even the Father; and therewith curse we men, which are made after the similitude of God.
[10] Out of the same mouth proceedeth blessing and cursing. My brethren, these things ought not so to be.

In verse seven, James continues to warn us about the tongue. He talks about **man's power and uniqueness to tame and control the beasts around us**. Man has conquered **all the animals on earth**. As great as man's ability is, there is one thing that he has not conquered. He has not conquered his own tongue. James tells us in verse eight that *"the tongue can no man tame."* The tongue is an unruly evil and it is full of deadly poison, a poison that can kill one or millions.

Here are some scriptures on the tongue and lying:

Psalm 34:13

Keep thy tongue from evil, and thy lips from speaking guile.

147

Psalm 140:3

They have sharpened their tongues like a serpent; adders' poison is under their lips. Selah.

Proverbs 13:3

He that keepeth his mouth keepeth his life: but he that openeth wide his lips shall have destruction.

Proverbs 21:22-23, 28

^{22} A wise man scaleth the city of the mighty, and casteth down the strength of the confidence thereof.
^{23} Whoso keepeth his mouth and his tongue keepeth his soul from troubles.
^{28} A false witness shall perish: but the man that heareth speaketh constantly.

James 1:26

If any man among you seem to be religious, and bridleth not his tongue, but deceiveth his own heart, this man's religion is vain.

1 Peter 3:10

For he that will love life, and see good days, let him refrain his tongue from evil, and his lips that they speak no guile:

Man, James tells us, will never be able to control his tongue. **Only one person can control our tongue, and that person is Jesus Christ.** When Jesus comes to live in our hearts, He **controls our tongue, if we will let Him.**

Barnes' Notes on the New Testament says:

> "With their tongues they have used deceit; the poison of asps is under their lips." Nothing would better describe the mischief that may be done by the tongue. There is no sting of a serpent that does so much evil in the world; there is no poison more deadly to the frame than the poison of the tongue is to the happiness of man. Who, for example, can stand before the power of the slanderer? What mischief can be done in society that can be compared with that which he, may do?

In verse nine, we read how man uses his tongue. He uses his tongue to **bless God, to praise Him and give Him glory**. Then he turns around and curses his fellow man. His mind is oblivious to what his tongue is doing. We might ask ourselves how a man or woman can think of themselves as a Christian when they **worship and praise and give honor to our heavenly Saviour and His Holy Father, our God**; then a few minutes later, curse their fellow man, calling him every ungodly thing he can think of. The answer is a very simple one. He cannot be a Christian and do these things. The devil has many people fooled by ungodly doctrine. As James so apply puts it, *"My brethren, these things ought not so to be."*

Are we so fickle, so inconstant, and so unreliable that we

have lost all control? The person who does not rely on God has very little self-control, and sadly, or so it seems, do most people that claim to be Christians. **If we have not totally surrendered our will, our emotions, and our temper to God, it is easy to lose all control.**

We must face facts. The tongue is unruly. However, it is out of the abundance of the heart that the mouth speaks. **When our heart is right, Jesus helps to bridle our tongue.** We are blessed in this life, we are blessed. There is an old chorus from years gone by that has fallen out of use, *Jesus Use Me,* by Jimmy Swaggart. It talks about being **blessed throughout your life.** It reminds us that we are blessed no matter what we face. Sometimes we need to be **reminded of the blessings God pours out on us**.

James 3:11-12

[11] Doth a fountain send forth at the same place sweet water and bitter?
[12] Can the fig tree, my brethren, bear olive berries? either a vine, figs? so can no fountain both yield salt water and fresh.

James gives us additional illustrations in verses eleven and twelve. Why is he giving us these illustrations? Because he wants to **gain the reader's attention**. James needs to prove a point for us to understand. If we will pay attention to nature, we will see certain fundamental laws **that cannot be broken**. A fig tree cannot **bear olive berries**; fresh water and salt water **cannot come out of the same spring**. It is not possible; it is **against the law of nature**. In light of this, James turns the illustration on us.

You cannot be a Christian and lie, cheat, or steal. This is not being Christ-like. You cannot be a Christian and hate your neighbor or covet his possessions. You cannot be a Christian and be a whoremonger, adulterer or a fornicator. You cannot be a Christian and take the Lord's name in vain or curse those you do not like. Regardless of what others may believe and teach, you **cannot be a Christian and continue to sin every day**. It goes **against the natural laws of God**. There is no such thing as "once you are saved, you are always saved," allowing you to commit sins regularly. **You cannot be a sinner and a Christian at the same time.**

Matthew 6:24

No man can serve two masters: for either he will hate the one, and love the other; or else he will hold to the one, and despise the other. Ye cannot serve God and mammon.

Luke 9:62

And Jesus said unto him, No man, having put his hand to the plough, and looking back, is fit for the kingdom of God.

James 3:13

Who is a wise man and endued with knowledge among you? let him shew out of a good conversation his works with meekness of wisdom.

Here James broaches the subject of wisdom or being wise.

151

Along with understanding, this wisdom **makes us a light shining into the darkness of sin**. Wisdom is the greatest thing we can acquire. Knowledge is a great thing to have; however; if you do not have the wisdom to use it, **then it offers you very little profit**.

We have all seen extremely smart people. They are a whiz at mathematics and/or brilliant in the knowledge of this world. However, they have no wisdom in how to use their knowledge, how to put it into practical application. **Wisdom is to be our main objective.** We are to pursue **wisdom and understanding** from God.

Webster's New World College Dictionary defines wisdom for us:

1. the quality of being wise; power of judging rightly and following the soundest course of action, based on knowledge, experience, understanding, etc.; good judgment; sagacity
2. learning; knowledge; erudition: the *wisdom* of the ages
3. [now rare] wise discourse or teaching

There are two different kinds of wisdom. There is a worldly wisdom, which is of this world. Worldly wisdom is frail and faulty. Then there is **spiritual wisdom that comes from God**, a wisdom that is **sound and faultless**. This wisdom is founded upon the Word of God.

1 Corinthians 1:19-21

[19] For it is written, I will destroy the wisdom of the wise, and will bring to nothing the understanding of the prudent.

152

²⁰ Where is the wise? where is the scribe? where is the disputer of this world? hath not God made foolish the wisdom of this world?

²¹ For after that in the wisdom of God the world by wisdom knew not God, it pleased God by the foolishness of preaching to save them that believe.

This worldly wisdom is carnal and is strictly worldly. It has **nothing to do with the heavenly**. Man believes in his wisdom and his knowledge. The world believes in itself and only itself. It will only use God for its own benefit, not because it believes in a heavenly God. When men lean upon their own understanding, they will always fail.

We all know that there is a **great amount of knowledge in this world**. Man has elevated his knowledge to a very high point, so high that much of the world has lost faith in a supreme being. All this world's knowledge does **little good without wisdom from above.** It is sad that our education system has decided to take God out of our schools and justice system.

What we need to do is **seek the wisdom and understanding** that comes from God. To a world that is ungodly, belief in God is foolishness. The world's elite desires to make people think and believe what they want. They want to do away with any reference to a deity, to God. However, Godly wisdom is real, just as God is real. Man may deny God. **Nevertheless, God is still real.**

1 Corinthians 2:5-8

⁵ That your faith should not stand in the wisdom of men, but in the power of God.

⁶ Howbeit we speak wisdom among them that are perfect: yet not the wisdom of this world, nor of the princes of this world, that come to nought:

⁷ But we speak the wisdom of God in a mystery, even the hidden wisdom, which God ordained before the world unto our glory:

⁸ Which none of the princes of this world knew: for had they known it, they would not have crucified the Lord of glory.

This Godly wisdom is **meek and gentle**. It boasts not of itself. It **exalts and praises God** forever and ever. What this world needs most of all, it rejects. It rejects Godly wisdom and knowledge combined with an understanding of the times. God desires that we **seek His face and His wisdom**. The scriptures tell us to **seek for wisdom and understanding**.

Psalm 51:6

Behold, thou desirest truth in the inward parts: and in the hidden part thou shalt make me to know wisdom.

Proverbs 3:13

Happy is the man that findeth wisdom, and the man that getteth understanding.

Proverbs 4:5-7

⁵ Get wisdom, get understanding: forget it not; neither decline from the words of my mouth.

154

⁶ Forsake her not, and she shall preserve thee: love her, and she shall keep thee.
⁷ Wisdom is the principal thing; therefore get wisdom: and with all thy getting get understanding.

James 3:14-16

¹⁴ But if ye have bitter envying and strife in your hearts, glory not, and lie not against the truth.
¹⁵ This wisdom descendeth not from above, but is earthly, sensual, devilish.
¹⁶ For where envying and strife is, there is confusion and every evil work.

James in this fourteenth verse begins to name part of the problems that affect mankind. First, he names bitter envying, which means **to desire what others have**. Many today are bitter in their hearts because of what other people possess and they do not have. They never stop to think that **most people work for what they have**. Some have worked much of their lives to own a home and car, and to put money in the bank.

We are living in a time when people declare that everyone should have the same things. If needs be, they want to **take from those who have and give it to those who do not**. It used to be that if you worked hard and made a success, people were glad for you. Now they want to take away what you have and give it to those who will not work and provide for themselves. They have bitter or hard feelings against others and desire their possessions. This causes strife in their hearts, and this strife causes people to resort to violence. We see it in the news and newspapers, of how people march in the streets. They get worked into a frenzy and damage cars, and they throw rocks and bricks through windows. They steal from shops, fight with those who do not agree with them and hurt others for the fun of it. Envying and strife only causes heartache and pain.

Next, James exhorts people to **stop lying about or against the truth**. How many times have we seen people who profess to be Christians, yet their lives do not portray what they profess? To say that you are a born-again child of God and then live like the devil does not put forth a good witness to those around you. I have never understood how a person who reads the Bible can believe that they are Christians when they lie, gossip, steal, curse and some even get drunk. Then, for example, when a person uses curse words and states, "Excuse my French." Do they not know that **there is a God who sees and hears** all?

We are judged by the world on **how we act, the things that we do, not just on the things we say**. There is a saying that is perfectly true and it goes like this: You can fool part of the people part of the time, and you can fool some of the people some of the time. However, you cannot fool all of the people all of the time. Think about it, are you trying to fool people? If so, you may get by with it for a while, but only for a while.

The world considers itself to be wise and filled with wisdom. Knowledge in this world **increases by leaps and bounds each year**. However, there is a world of difference between knowledge and wisdom. The world's wisdom amounts to very little, for it is carnal. However, **heavenly wisdom which comes from above is true, holy, and beneficial**. As long as we **lean upon the Lord and obey His will**, He will guide us **in truth and holiness**.

In verse sixteen, James makes a profound statement. He

reminds us that **confusion is brought about by evil**. Envying and strife is an everyday happening in this world, since the god of this world is the devil. Evil works in the lives of people who do not have a personal relationship with Jesus Christ. Envying and strife bring sorrow, pain, heartache and confusion in lives. Is it any wonder that the world is in the shape it is in?

James 3:17-18

[17] But the wisdom that is from above is first pure, then peaceable, gentle, and easy to be intreated, full of mercy and good fruits, without partiality, and without hypocrisy. [18] And the fruit of righteousness is sown in peace of them that make peace.

These last two verses tell us of the wisdom that comes from above, the wisdom that God gives to those who ask and seek for it.

Isaiah 11:2

And the spirit of the LORD shall rest upon him, the spirit of wisdom and understanding, the spirit of counsel and might, the spirit of knowledge and of the fear of the LORD.

Romans 11:33

O the depth of the riches both of the wisdom and knowledge of God! how unsearchable are his judgments, and his ways past finding out!

1 Corinthians 1:25

Because the foolishness of God is wiser than men; and the weakness of God is stronger than men.

Job 28:28

And unto man he said, Behold, the fear of the Lord, that is wisdom; and to depart from evil is understanding.

Proverbs 4:7

Wisdom is the principal thing; therefore get wisdom: and with all thy getting get understanding.

The wisdom that comes from God is pure. It is undefiled by the things of this world. It is **clean, faultless, unmixed and untangled** by any evil or impure thing. In addition, God's wisdom is **peaceable, gentle, and easy to be entreated**.

Barnes' Notes on the New Testament says:

> The meaning here is, that the first and immediate effect of religion is not on the intellect, to make it more enlightened; or on the imagination, to make it more discursive and brilliant; or on the memory and judgment, to make them clearer and stronger; but it is to *purify* the heart, to make the man upright, inoffensive, and good. This passage should not be applied, as it often is, to the *doctrines* of religion, as if it were the first duty of a

church to keep itself free from errors in doctrine, and that this ought to be sought even in preference to the maintenance of peace-as if it meant that in doctrine a church should be *"first* pure, *then* peaceable;"* but it should be applied *to the individual consciences of men,* as showing the effect of religion on the heart and life. The *first* thing which it produces is to make the man himself pure and good;

The wisdom of God is full of mercy and good fruits, **without partiality or hypocrisy**. God is full of mercy and love, and **His grace is sufficient for us**. The child of God's life is full of good fruits or works; without **any kind of partiality and treating all the same**; and without any hypocrisy. As Christians, we must be **truthful and straightforward in all that we do**.

Verse eighteen tells us that peacemakers **sow the fruit of righteousness in peace**. As we study the scriptures, they tell us that we are to **walk in righteousness before God**. You may say, "Wait a minute, the Bible states there is none righteous, no not one." This is true. However, a Christian **does not walk in his own righteousness**. He walks in the **righteousness of Jesus Christ**, and as Christ lives in us, so does Christ's righteousness **show forth through us**.

As I close this chapter, we look around us and can easily tell that the world has become pleasure mad. People have given themselves over to the hunger of the flesh. The unsaved have no control or do not wish to control their desires. They seek for and find ways to justify the things they desire to do.

Because of men like Sigmund Freud who have made the irresponsible actions of people excusable, they blame all their actions upon others, taking no responsibility for themselves. What is even worse, the world has begun to swallow these lies. James goes on to say that this wisdom is devilish. It was concocted in hell and is meant for the destruction of mankind. On the other side, **there is a Godly wisdom, which is pure**. It is founded upon God and His power. James tells us that it is **peaceable and full of mercy**. It produces **good fruit without any kind of partiality**, and best of all, it is **honest without hypocrisy**. It is not of this world, but it is **of God and is sent down to His people** to make our lives better as we walk with Him. Like verse eighteen states, *"And the fruit of righteousness is sown in peace of them that make peace."*

Chapter 3 Review Questions

1. What problem does James deal with in the first verse?

_____

_____

_____

2. Why is an unqualified teacher a danger to the true gospel

message?

_____

_____

_____

3. What are we to do when we learn we have offended someone?

_____

_____

_____

4. What does the Bible say about the tongue?

_____

_____

_____

5. As we study the illustration of the ship, it shows us that Jesus is

_____

_____

6. Why should we guard the words we speak?

_____

_____

_____

7. In verse eight, James tells us what about the tongue?

_____

_____

_____

8. Who is able to control our tongue?

_____

_____

_____

9. What happens out of the abundance of the heart?

_____

_____

10. In nature, there are certain fundamental laws which cannot be broken. What illustrations does James use in verses eleven and twelve?

_____

_____

_____

11. Why should wisdom be the Christian's main objective to acquire?

_____

_____

12. Are you trying to fool people around you? There is an old saying that states that you can fool part of the people part of the time and some of the people some of the time, however . . .

_____

_____

13. The wisdom that comes from above is what?

_____

_____

14. A Christian does not walk in his own righteousness. How is a Christian supposed to walk?

_____

_____

_____

Chapter 4

From whence come wars and fightings among you? come they not hence, even of your lusts that war in your members?

James starts this chapter with a question. *"From whence come wars and fightings among you?"* Then he answers it to bring us back to an ugly truth. Those wars come from within us. They are the results of the envying and bitterness that lives within our hearts. Man has never learned to live in peace one with another, and sometimes he cannot even live with himself.

Countries cannot get along with each other. States, companies, even neighbors cannot get along together. There are even troubles in the churches of God. When man yields to the carnal, there is always trouble. **In Christ Jesus, there is peace and contentment.**

The Wiersbe Bible Commentary: NT says:

When you examine some of the early churches,

165

you discover that they had their share of disagreements. The members of the Corinthian church were competing with each other in the public meetings, and even suing each other in court (1 Cor. 6:1-8; 14:23-40). The Galatian believers were "biting and devouring" one another (Gal. 5:15). Paul had to admonish the Ephesians to cultivate spiritual unity (Eph. 4:1-16), and even his beloved church at Philippi had problems: two women could not get along with each other (Phil. 4:1-3).

James mentioned several different kinds of disagreements among the saints.

Trouble in the church is the worst kind of trouble there is, because it involves the saints, the children of God. When there is trouble in the church, the devil tries to make sure everyone around knows about it. He does this to bring shame upon the church and the saints.

We all have a **God-given desire to achieve**, and there is **nothing wrong in this**. The wrong comes when we are driven to achieve at the expense of others. When we are willing to lie, cheat and do whatever it takes to come out on top, we have crossed the line and sinned. We all want to be recognized for our achievements, **for our good works**. We forget that we are to do our good works **and not boast about them, for God sees and knows all**.

James 4:2-3

2 Ye lust, and have not: ye kill, and desire to have, and cannot obtain: ye fight and war, yet ye have not, because

ye ask not.
3 Ye ask, and receive not, because ye ask amiss, that ye
may consume it upon your lusts.

James brings home the truth of God's Word about the worldly minded. He states that *"ye lust and have not; ye kill and desire to have, and cannot obtain."* **This is a perfect picture of the world today.** Sadly, the church is beginning to follow the same path as the world. Lust is running rampant in the world of today. Men and women are lusting after each other as never before. People are lusting after worldly possessions to heap unto themselves. In all this lusting, only one in ten thousand or more get what they desire. This only causes the rest to be that much worse in trying to satisfy their lust.

Mankind is a slave to lust and desire, and this desire to have more and more possessions is ruling people's lives and everything that they say and do. **Without Jesus Christ, we are slaves to the world, chained by sin,** in bondage to the devil and his will. Most people wonder what has gone wrong with this world. People are killing each other at an unbelievable rate. Murders, rapes, violence of all kinds. The world is in a state of chaos. The only hope the world has is in Jesus Christ, our Lord. The world has forgotten the Ten Commandments and changed them into the ten suggestions. The world wants no commandments placed upon it.

The Lord tells us that we **have not because we ask not**; however, we must remember that the Lord **was not talking to the world** when He said this. He was talking to the saints. If you, as a child of God, ask of God, then **God can answer your prayers.** James states in verse three a very profound truth that most Christians never think about. *"Ye ask, and receive not, because ye*

167

ask amiss, that ye may consume it upon your lust."

Most people never read this verse. They pray for **all manner of things, some good and some bad**. As the scripture states, they prayed **out of their own lust**. These prayers God will not answer because of His love for us. Out of the ignorance of God's Word, people do many things that are not pleasing to God. **If you know the Word of God, it is much easier to not make simple mistakes.**

Ignorance of God's Word will not be acceptable when we stand before God, because we have the Bible at our disposal. If a person does not own one, they can buy a New Testament for a few dollars, and in this age there are apps for phones and tablets that are free; you can find a copy of the Bible on the internet. Therefore, there is **no excuse for being ignorant of God's Word**.

Let me remind you of what the scripture tells us about God. It states that it is a **fearful thing to fall into the hands of a living God**.

Hebrews 10:30-31

> [30] *For we know him that hath said, Vengeance belongeth unto me, I will recompense, saith the Lord. And again, The Lord shall judge his people.*
> [31] *It is a fearful thing to fall into the hands of the living God.*

We are living in an age where most of this generation is ignorant of God. Many have never set foot in a church. This in no way will be an excuse before God. **We are responsible for ourselves when we stand before God.** No one can make you miss heaven but you.

When we surrender our lives to Christ and become born again, we have the right to **take our needs and petitions before the Lord**. However, this still does not give us the right to pray for things from our lustful nature, **just because we want them**.

Psalm 66:18

If I regard iniquity in my heart, the Lord will not hear me:

When we let lust have control, we begin to covet what others have and make plans to have the same things as others regardless of the cost.

The Wiersbe Bible Commentary: NT clarifies this:

> "Thou shalt not covet" is the last of God's Ten Commandments, but its violation can make us break all of the other nine! Covetousness can make a person murder, tell lies, dishonor his parents, commit adultery, and in one way or another violate all of God's moral law. Selfish living and selfish praying always lead to war. If there is war on the inside, there will ultimately be war on the outside.
>
> People who are at war with themselves because of selfish desires are always unhappy people. They never enjoy life. Instead of being thankful for the blessings they do have, they complain about the blessings they do not have. They cannot get along with other people because they are always envying others for what they have and do. They are always looking for that "magic something" that will

change their lives, when the real problem is within their own hearts.

Are you thankful for your blessings? On the other hand, are you blaming God because you do not have what others have? If you are not satisfied, it is time to **turn everything over to Christ**. Because only Jesus can **give you a satisfied heart and mind**. The peace of mind that Jesus gives is **worth everything we give** over to Him.

James 4:4-5

⁴ Ye adulterers and adulteresses, know ye not that the friendship of the world is enmity with God? whosoever therefore will be a friend of the world is the enemy of God. ⁵ Do ye think that the scripture saith in vain, The spirit that dwelleth in us lusteth to envy?

James continues in these two verses **about the faults of men and women in the churches and outside the churches**. He begins by saying, *"Ye adulterers and adulteresses."* In the scriptures we read much about this offence. Adultery was a **very serious sin in the Old Testament** and was punishable by death.

The John Phillips Commentary Series says:

I once heard Dr. Adrian Rodgers, pastor of the great Bellevue Baptist Church in Memphis, Tennessee, say, "A man committing adultery says to his children: 'Your mother is not worth much, and your father is a cheat and a liar. Honor is not as important as pleasure, and my satisfaction is

170

more important than you.'"

Men and women who yield to the flesh and to the fleshly lust that besets us are wrecked upon the rocks of sin. God condemns adultery in both the natural flesh and the spiritual. As bad as adultery is in the flesh, adultery in the spiritual is even worse.

When we accept Jesus Christ as our personal Saviour, we become **a part of the Bride of Christ**. We become committed to Jesus Christ; scripture says **we are espoused to Jesus**. When a Christian begins to sin, they are for all practical purposes committing adultery. You have broken the covenant you made with God on the day of your salvation. What you are saying to God is that your desires and wants are more important than He is. We see people everywhere who say that they are Christians. However, their heart's desires are for the pleasures of the world and what it can give.

James goes on to inform us that the friendship of the world is enmity with God. I have heard preachers say that the church must be friends with the world, if we are to reach them for Christ. However, I still hold that we cannot help the world when we descend to their level. The churches are to **lift the sinners up into the presence of God**, not stoop down to their level of sin. Jesus said, **"When I be lifted up, I will draw all men to me."**

John 12:32

> *And I, if I be lifted up from the earth, will draw all men unto me.*

We cannot afford to be friends with the world. God considers friendship with the world the same as committing

171

adultery. The born-again child of God walks in this world; however, he is **not a part of the world**. You may ask how this can be. When we surrender our lives to Christ, we **renounce this world and all that it has**. We renounce our citizenship to this world, and as for as the world is concerned, we are aliens. We have **changed our citizenship to become citizens of the kingdom of God**. Romans tell us that to be carnally minded is death. The scriptures in Romans chapter 8 are very plain and to the point.

Romans 8:5-8

> *[5] For they that are after the flesh do mind the things of the flesh; but they that are after the Spirit the things of the Spirit.*
> *[6] For to be carnally minded is death; but to be spiritually minded is life and peace.*
> *[7] Because the carnal mind is enmity against God: for it is not subject to the law of God, neither indeed can be.*
> *[8] So then they that are in the flesh cannot please God.*

We must always remember that if we are friends with the world, then we are the enemies of God. James makes it even clearer in verse five when he writes, "Do you think that the scriptures tell us in vain that the spirit of man that lives in our bodies lusts and causes us to envy and covet?"

James 4:5

Do ye think that the scripture saith in vain, The spirit that dwelleth in us lusteth to envy?

It is the desire of Jesus Christ and our God most high that **all men might be saved everywhere**. Nevertheless, this will not be so, for man's will is strong. You can throw a drowning man a life preserver. However, if he refuses to use it, then his death is upon his own head. **Jesus is our spiritual life preserver given to us by God.** If a soul refuses to take advantage of God's gift, then they can blame only themselves when they stand before the living God.

James 4:6-7

⁶ But he giveth more grace. Wherefore he saith, God resisteth the proud, but giveth grace unto the humble.
⁷ Submit yourselves therefore to God. Resist the devil, and he will flee from you.

James declares in verse six that God will **give more grace to His saints** when they are being tried and tested by the enemy (old Satan). If you will remember, Paul had a thorn in the flesh. No one knows for sure what it was. Scripture tells us that Paul prayed and sought God, asking Him to take away his thorn in the flesh. God's reply to Paul was to tell him that **His grace was sufficient for him whatever the problem might be**. This is the same answer God gives us today, that **His grace is sufficient for all our needs**.

2 Corinthians 12:9-10

⁹ And he said unto me, My grace is sufficient for thee: for my strength is made perfect in weakness. Most gladly therefore will I rather glory in my infirmities, that the

power of Christ may rest upon me.
[10] Therefore I take pleasure in infirmities, in reproaches, in necessities, in persecutions, in distresses for Christ's sake: for when I am weak, then am I strong.

The problem is when people who claim to be Christians **refuse to accept what God tells them**. In addition, the devil jumps in and tells people that God does not really love them, because if He did, He would answer their prayers and give them what they want. I have said this before, and I will repeat it again. People want an **instant God who gives an instant answer** to their prayers. Why? It is because we live in an instant world. We have instant food, instant banking on our computers and telephones, and instant communication via cell phones. Therefore, people who are used to things being instant want an instant God.

I will be the first to tell you that **God is a constant help in the time of trouble**. However, we must remember that God is never early. On the other hand, He is never late. He is always **right on time**. What am I saying? I am saying that God **moves in His own time and not on our time**. We must learn that the world, when they choose to believe in God, believe that God is old-fashioned. They never stop to realize that God moves by His time and not ours. **God is the one who is in control.** There is a song called *The Old-Fashioned Meeting,* and part of it goes like this:

> 'Twas an old-fashioned meeting, in an old-fashioned place,
> Where some old-fashioned people had some old-fashioned grace:
> As an old-fashioned sinner I began to pray,

174

And God heard me, and saved me in the old-fashioned way.

So, child of God, we serve a God that the world claims is old-fashioned. A God they no longer need, for they think that to believe in God is using a crutch to lean on. Well, as far as I am concerned, they can call believing in God a crutch. I call it being wise; for **Jesus is my Saviour, my rod, and my staff**. He is my **keeper, my King, and my Redeemer**. I will **lean upon Him all the days of my life**.

If you are too proud to lean upon the Lord, then you are **too proud for your own good**. James tells us a truth that we will do well to never forget, that **God resists the proud**. Pride will lead a person to destruction. It will lead to bad choices. It causes people to fail others and most of all to fail themselves. The scripture, the Word of God, tells us that **pride goes before a fall**.

Proverbs 6:16-19

> *16 These six things doth the LORD hate: yea, seven are an abomination unto him:*
> *17 A proud look, a lying tongue, and hands that shed innocent blood,*
> *18 An heart that deviseth wicked imaginations, feet that be swift in running to mischief,*
> *19 A false witness that speaketh lies, and he that soweth discord among brethren.*

Yet, to those who are humble, **God gives grace**, for His grace is **sufficient for us, no matter what the devil throws at us**.

The scripture gives us the way to defeat Satan if we will use it. In verse seven, it states that we must **submit ourselves to the service of the Lord our God**. This sounds easy to do. However, it is not that easy. Our human nature resists submission to anyone or anything. Yet, submission to our Lord is **vital in serving God**. Our self-will and pride keep us from receiving God's best. To receive the blessings of God, we must **yield ourselves to God's will**. In the scriptures, we read the following:

1 Samuel 15:22

> *And Samuel said, Hath the LORD as great delight in burnt offerings and sacrifices, as in obeying the voice of the LORD? Behold, to obey is better than sacrifice, and to hearken than the fat of rams.*

Acts 5:29

> *Then Peter and the other apostles answered and said, We ought to obey God rather than men.*

As long as we resist the devil and submit ourselves to God, the devil will take his bag of tricks and flee from us. In the name of Jesus, we have the victory.

The John Phillips Commentary Series tells us:

> To accept God's grace, we must lay aside all pride and come as a repentant sinner to the foot of the cross. He "giveth grace unto the humble," adds James. God's grace does not end with our salva-

176

tion; it provides us with all that we need for the journey home. God's grace set Egypt's captives free. But God not only put His people under the blood but also marched them out of the house of bondage, brought them through the water, and turned their faces toward the Promised Land. Did they need water? He brought it flowing from the riven rock. Did they need food? He sent them bread from heaven. Were they assailed by foes? He gave them victory. Did they need to know which way to go? He marched before them. Did they need protection from the smiting sun and staring moon? He spread a cloudy canopy over one and all. Did they need to cross a river? He smote it so that it parted before them. Were the walls of Jericho too great and tall and strong? He knocked them down.

It was all of grace for them. It is all of grace for us. So wrote John Newton in his hymn "Amazing Grace":

'Twas grace that taught my heart to fear,
And grace my fears relieved;
How precious did that grace appear
The hour I first believed!
Through many dangers, toils, and snares,
I have already come;
'Tis grace hath brought me safe thus far,
And grace will see me home.

By grace, we are **saved through faith in Jesus Christ our**

Lord. Jesus is **our deliver, our redeemer, our protector, our soon coming king**.

Ephesians 2:5, 8

> *⁵ Even when we were dead in sins, hath quickened us together with Christ, (by grace ye are saved;)*
> *⁸ For by grace are ye saved through faith; and that not of yourselves: it is the gift of God:*

Ephesians 4:7

> *But unto every one of us is given grace according to the measure of the gift of Christ.*

James 4:8-10

> *⁸ Draw nigh to God, and he will draw nigh to you. Cleanse your hands, ye sinners; and purify your hearts, ye double minded.*
> *⁹ Be afflicted, and mourn, and weep: let your laughter be turned to mourning, and your joy to heaviness.*
> *¹⁰ Humble yourselves in the sight of the Lord, and he shall lift you up.*

Verse eight tells man that God's desire is to be close to Him. James writes, *"Draw nigh to God, and he will draw nigh to you."* When we were sinners, God was a long way off. However, that distance is **done away with when we come to Jesus** and ask Him to forgive us of our sins. At that moment, Jesus **comes into our hearts to set up His abode and live there**.

As long as we walk with Jesus, He will **walk with us**. He

will **dwell within us all the days** of our lives. The only way that Jesus will leave us is if we walk away from Him and begin to sin. The spirit of God and Jesus will not have anything to do with sin. The spirit of light cannot and will not have anything to do with the spirit of darkness. When a Christian begins to sin, the spirit of Christ leaves that person because they love darkness more than light. Going back to verse four, the scripture teaches us that God considers Christians who sin to be adulterers and adulteresses. Remember, the Bible was written to Christians, not to sinners.

Galatians 4:9

> *But now, after that ye have known God, or rather are known of God, how turn ye again to the weak and beggarly elements, whereunto ye desire again to be in bondage?*

Hebrews 7:19

> *For the law made nothing perfect, but the bringing in of a better hope did; by the which we draw nigh unto God.*

Once again, we touch on **whether there is such a thing as eternal salvation**. I stress that there is no eternal salvation. A man or woman can (and many do) walk away from God and go back into the world of sin. Thus, they lose that which God gave to them, their salvation. They **become backsliders, lost, away from God**. Scriptures to prove this are as follows:

Ezekiel 18:24

> *But when the righteous turneth away from his righteous-*

ness, and committeth iniquity, and doeth according to all the abominations that the wicked man doeth, shall he live? All his righteousness that he hath done shall not be mentioned: in his trespass that he hath trespassed, and in his sin that he hath sinned, in them shall he die.

Matthew 7:21-23

21 Not every one that saith unto me, Lord, Lord, shall enter into the kingdom of heaven; but he that doeth the will of my Father which is in heaven.
22 Many will say to me in that day, Lord, Lord, have we not prophesied in thy name? and in thy name have cast out devils? and in thy name done many wonderful works?
23 And then will I profess unto them, I never knew you: depart from me, ye that work iniquity.

Matthew 24:10-13

10 And then shall many be offended, and shall betray one another, and shall hate one another.
11 And many false prophets shall rise, and shall deceive many.
12 And because iniquity shall abound, the love of many shall wax cold.
13 But he that shall endure unto the end, the same shall be saved.

Matthew 25:1-13

1 Then shall the kingdom of heaven be likened unto ten virgins, which took their lamps, and went forth to meet the bridegroom.

² And five of them were wise, and five were foolish.

³ They that were foolish took their lamps, and took no oil with them:

⁴ But the wise took oil in their vessels with their lamps.

⁵ While the bridegroom tarried, they all slumbered and slept.

⁶ And at midnight there was a cry made, Behold, the bridegroom cometh; go ye out to meet him.

⁷ Then all those virgins arose, and trimmed their lamps.

⁸ And the foolish said unto the wise, Give us of your oil; for our lamps are gone out.

⁹ But the wise answered, saying, Not so; lest there be not enough for us and you: but go ye rather to them that sell, and buy for yourselves.

¹⁰ And while they went to buy, the bridegroom came; and they that were ready went in with him to the marriage: and the door was shut.

¹¹ Afterward came also the other virgins, saying, Lord, Lord, open to us.

¹² But he answered and said, Verily I say unto you, I know you not.

¹³ Watch therefore, for ye know neither the day nor the hour wherein the Son of man cometh.

Luke 8:11

Now the parable is this: The seed is the word of God.

Luke 9:62

And Jesus said unto him, No man, having put his hand to

the plough, and looking back, is fit for the kingdom of God.

Luke 11:24-26

[24] When the unclean spirit is gone out of a man, he walketh through dry places, seeking rest; and finding none, he saith, I will return unto my house whence I came out.
[25] And when he cometh, he findeth it swept and garnished.
[26] Then goeth he, and taketh to him seven other spirits more wicked than himself; and they enter in, and dwell there: and the last state of that man is worse than the first.

Galatians 1:6

I marvel that ye are so soon removed from him that called you into the grace of Christ unto another gospel:

Galatians 4:8-9

[8] Howbeit then, when ye knew not God, ye did service unto them which by nature are no gods.
[9] But now, after that ye have known God, or rather are known of God, how turn ye again to the weak and beggarly elements, whereunto ye desire again to be in bondage?

1 Timothy 4:1-2

[1] Now the Spirit speaketh expressly, that in the latter times some shall depart from the faith, giving heed to seducing spirits, and doctrines of devils;

² Speaking lies in hypocrisy; having their conscience seared with a hot iron;

Hebrews 10:38

Now the just shall live by faith: but if any man draw back, my soul shall have no pleasure in him.

Revelation 2:4-5

⁴ Nevertheless I have somewhat against thee, because thou hast left thy first love.
⁵ Remember therefore from whence thou art fallen, and repent, and do the first works; or else I will come unto thee quickly, and will remove thy candlestick out of his place, except thou repent.

When a person walks away from God, they are once more lost. If they should die while away from God, they are forever lost, separated from God. I know it sounds good to say that once you give your heart and life to God, your soul is sealed away from sin, and that what you do after the point of salvation does not concern your soul; however, it does. I believe that if sin condemned your soul before your salvation, that same sin, if committed, will also condemn your soul after you are saved. Sin is sin, and if God does not judge Christians who sin, He cannot judge sinners for committing sin. The scripture tells us that **God is no respecter of persons**.

Acts 10:34

Then Peter opened his mouth, and said, Of a truth I

perceive that God is no respecter of persons:

Draw nigh unto God. Seek His lovely face, call upon Him, and make Him the light of your life. Obey His Word. Be like the psalmist David, a person after God's own heart. David purposed in his heart to serve the Lord and make God a light unto his path.

Psalm 4:6

There be many that say, Who will shew us any good? LORD, lift thou up the light of thy countenance upon us.

Psalm 119:105

Thy word is a lamp unto my feet, and a light unto my path.

Psalm 119:130

The entrance of thy words giveth light; it giveth understanding unto the simple.

Then Solomon wrote the following words:

Proverbs 4:18

But the path of the just is as the shining light, that shineth more and more unto the perfect day.

Proverbs 6:23

For the commandment is a lamp; and the law is light; and

reproofs of instruction are the way of life:

Have you ever heard the illustration of an old couple driving down the highway? The wife asks her husband, "John, do you remember when we were young and going together?" John answers, "How could I ever forget?" She asks, "Do you remember how close together we used to sit back then?" John replies, "Yes, I do." Then she asks, "Whatever happened to us that we don't sit like that anymore?" John thought about it for a minute and then said, "I haven't moved."

If any moving is done, **it is us and not God**. As long as we walk in the light of God's countenance, **everything is all right**. However, when we begin to move away from God, we begin to get into trouble. What does God's Word tell us in the last part of this verse? *"Cleanse your hands, ye sinners and purify your hearts, ye double minded."* In other words, we are to **repent and to ask for forgiveness from God** for being stupid. God expects us to do our **first works over again**. We need to experience the **initial joy of our salvation one more time** to build a Christ-like mind.

In verse nine, we read: *"Be afflicted, and mourn, and weep."* God is serious about sin, because God hates sin. There are many today in our churches that outwardly submit to God, while inwardly they are rebellious and full of pride. Self-will reigns in their lives. It is a good thing to **clean up the outside and outwardly submit to God**. Nevertheless, it does very little good if we do not **submit and clean the inward man**. The cleaning of the inward man is the **most important thing that we can do**. For, if the inward man is submissive, the **outward man will change to reflect the inner man**.

One of the main changes in the church today is that of

185

tolerance. The church has become too tolerant of sin. It is time that the church once more begins to **preach on sin and what will happen to sinners**. When we invite the sinner to worship services, something is wrong in the church when they are comfortable sitting on the pew. I do not mean that we are not to be friendly. We are to **be friendly and show them a Christ-like love**. However, we are not to give them the impression that we approve of their sinful ways and lifestyle.

Sinners must come to the realization that **they are lost and on their way to an eternity without God**. The church that is tolerant of sin is doing the sinner a great injustice. It must preach the **Word of God just as it is**. God cannot bring conviction to a sinner's heart if they do not know the truth. I know that the trend is to preach **only the love of God** and not to preach on hell, the abode of the sinful soul. It is a shame that too many pastors view leading their churches as a job and nothing more. Pastoring a church is a God-given calling and not just an occupation.

Today, many pastors heading mainstream churches have missed God's calling. A pastor must be **God-called to do the work that God wants done**. The devil is loose in our churches and has played havoc, encouraging acceptance of the homosexual lifestyle as perfectly all right; couples living together without marriage; and drinking, cursing and fornication as acceptable and not a sin. What a terrible time we live in!

In verse ten we read that the key to pleasing God is to *"Humble yourselves in the sight of the Lord."* Our reasonable place is to be **humble before God and thankful for His forgiving grace** and redemption from sin. For it was against God that we sinned. We need to be **humble like David before God**.

Psalm 51:1-4 & 15-17

¹ Have mercy upon me, O God, according to thy loving-kindness: according unto the multitude of thy tender mercies blot out my transgressions.

² Wash me throughly from mine iniquity, and cleanse me from my sin.

³ For I acknowledge my transgressions: and my sin is ever before me.

⁴ Against thee, thee only, have I sinned, and done this evil in thy sight: that thou mightest be justified when thou speakest, and be clear when thou judgest.

¹⁵ O Lord, open thou my lips; and my mouth shall shew forth thy praise.

¹⁶ For thou desirest not sacrifice; else would I give it: thou delightest not in burnt offering.

¹⁷ The sacrifices of God are a broken spirit: a broken and a contrite heart, O God, thou wilt not despise.

As we humble ourselves before the Lord and give Him praise and worship, He will **lift up our spirits to heavenly heights** in His presence. Scripture teaches us that **God inhabits the praises of His people**, for we are a spiritual Israel. Worship Him for He is **worthy of all praise and glory**.

Psalm 22:3

But thou art holy, O thou that inhabitest the praises of Israel.

James 4:11-12

¹¹ Speak not evil one of another, brethren. He that speaketh evil of his brother, and judgeth his brother, speaketh evil of the law, and judgeth the law: but if thou judge the law, thou art not a doer of the law, but a judge. [12] There is one lawgiver, who is able to save and to destroy: who art thou that judgest another?

To begin this eleventh verse, I want to quote from *Barnes' Notes.*

Barnes' Notes on the New Testament says:

> It is not known to whom the apostle here particularly refers, nor is it necessary to know. It is probable that among those whom he addressed there were some who were less circumspect in regard to speaking of others than they should be, and perhaps this evil prevailed. There are few communities where such an injunction would not be proper at any time, and few churches where some might not be found to whom the exhortation would be appropriate.

James is speaking of one of the biggest problems in the church and the world: when people **talk about and judge others**. In Matthew 7:1, we read: *"Judge not, that ye be not judged."* We see people judge others by the kind of house they live in, by how much money they make, by the way that they dress or by the kind of car they drive. They do not know many of these people; nevertheless, they judge them anyway.

A Christian once said, "Well, if I am telling the truth, I am not speaking evil about anyone." However, this is a wrong attitude. You cannot talk about a person **without doing them**

harm unless you are praising them for their good works. What you are saying may be true, yet to tell others causes those who do not know them to pass judgement upon their brother or sister in the church (and the same applies to those outside the church).

Jesus tells us to **love one another, to love our brothers and sisters in the Lord**. Even to love our neighbors as ourselves. We are not to judge them, for we are not to be the judge of one another. God is our judge, the **judge of everyone**. To sit in judgment is to presume to **take God's place and to sin against God**.

Gossip and tale bearing are just as sinful as cursing, backbiting and other sins of the tongue. The tongue can kill, or the tongue can speak life, according to how it is used. Another way to say it, who is in control of our tongue, the devil or Jesus, our Lord and Saviour?

As verse twelve states, there is **only one lawgiver and one judge**. His name is God, and **only He is able to save and to destroy**. Who is man that he would presume to be God? Yet God is **mindful of man, for man is His creation**.

Psalm 8:4-5

> *[4] What is man, that thou art mindful of him? and the son of man, that thou visitest him?*
> *[5] For thou hast made him a little lower than the angels, and hast crowned him with glory and honour.*

James 4:13-17

> *[3] Go to now, ye that say, To day or to morrow we will go into such a city, and continue there a year, and buy and sell, and get gain:*

189

*14 Whereas ye know not what shall be on the morrow. For
what is your life? It is even a vapour, that appeareth for a
little time, and then vanisheth away.
15 For that ye ought to say, If the Lord will, we shall live,
and do this, or that.
16 But now ye rejoice in your boastings: all such rejoicing
is evil.
17 Therefore to him that knoweth to do good, and doeth it
not, to him it is sin.*

The apostle in verse thirteen begins a **new subject on how
people think and what they say**. They say, "I am going to go
here or there or I am going to do this or that," without any thought
of what might happen in the future. It is ok to make plans.
However, at the same time we need to **put our confidence and
trust in the Lord and His providence** for our lives. We need to
say, "The Lord permitting."

Verse fourteen carries this thought even further by saying
that we do not know what is going to happen when tomorrow
comes. Then the apostle asks a very profound question. "*For what
is your life?*" The apostle answers his own question. "*It is even a
vapour, that appeareth for a little time and then vanishes away.*"
When we think of a vapor, we think of a mist. It **appears out of
seemingly nowhere and then vanishes away**. We do not have
the promise of tomorrow, whether **we should live or die**.

Verse fifteen states that we should say, "If it is the Lord's
will, we will do this or that, for we do not know what tomorrow
holds." Only God knows, so we must **put our faith in God**.

Verse sixteen tells us that we need to be very careful about
boasting. A person who goes about boasting is full of self, full of
pride, full of evil. He promotes an image of how great he is, but in

190

reality fools no one.

Verse seventeen is self-explanatory and means just what it says. *"Therefore to him that knoweth to do good, and doeth it not, to him it is sin."*

Chapter 4 Review Questions

1. What is the ugly truth that James brings us back to?

_____

_____

_____

2. What does James say about the worldly-minded?

_____

_____

_____

3. Why has the world changed the Ten Commandments into the

ten suggestions?

_____

_____

_____

4. What does James tell us is the reason why many prayers are

never answered?

_____

_____

5. Why will ignorance of God's Word not be an accepted excuse when we stand before God?

_____

_____

_____

6. What is a Christian doing spiritually when he begins to sin?

_____

_____

7. Explain your answer to question #6.

_____

_____

8. What kind of God do people want in this instant age of ours?

_____

_____

9. How does verse seven tell us to put the devil to flight?

_____

_____

_____

10. The spirit of Christ or the spirit of light cannot and will not have anything to with . . .

_____

11. When we clean up the inner man, what happens to the outer man?

_____

_____

_____

12. Why is it important for sinners to realize that they are lost?

_____

_____

_____

13. What did psalmist David say in Psalms 51:16-17? Please write the two verses out. (Continue onto p. 195.)

_____

_____

_____

_____

14. To whom was the Bible written?

_____

_____

_____

15. What must we do, since we do not know what tomorrow

holds?

_____

_____

_____

Chapter 5

I am beginning this chapter with an introduction, because I would like us to look at certain things before we begin. We will be touching on this introduction as we go through the verses. The first main topic is about **people having troubles**, and the other main topic is **about prayer**.

Most of us have the same problem when it comes to money. Money, it seems, is always **saying goodbye to us**, since we seem never to be able to keep hold of it. We use it to pay bills like car payments, house payments, insurance, utilities, food and gasoline. Money seems to **pass right through our hands**, and very little seems to remain with us. The rich men in the first part of this chapter seem to have been able to acquire and hold on to their money. Money had become so important to them that it **became like their god**.

Please do not get the wrong idea. Being rich in this world's goods is not a sin. Many of God's faithful followers were very rich men. Men like **Abraham, who was a very rich man**, yet he walked with God. God made Abraham a promise. **Because of his faithfulness, Abraham's seed would become a great nation** and the whole earth would be blessed because of him.

What James was concerned about was the spirit of

selfishness that the wayward rich seem to possess. Another thing is what the unscrupulous rich do to obtain their riches. I have seen how some wealthy people, wanting to acquire more and more, take advantage of others. They lie, defraud, sometimes outright steal and cheat to keep gaining riches.

Next let us look at prayer. Prayer is not something to be used for selfish gain. Prayer is a **means by which we talk to God**, telling Him how much we **love Him and thank Him** for all He has done for us. It is a means of giving God **praise and glory for His many, many blessings**. Then, after we have given thanks for all that God has done for us, we bring our needs and petitions before the Lord. Some call it a time of airing our grievances before God. Call it what you will, **God answers these prayers.**

God meets our needs, heals our bodies, and is our burden bearer. Nevertheless, most Christians do not understand prayer. It is not a time for us to go before the Lord and say give me this and that. Prayer is a time of **worship and praise, a time of communication between God and us**. We talk to God, and then we **listen and God talks to us**. Too many Christians do all the talking and none of the listening.

James 5:1

Go to now, ye rich men, weep and howl for your miseries
that shall come upon you.

James begins this first verse with a warning to the rich, telling them to weep and howl because of God's judgement that was soon to come upon them because of how they have treated others. The rich can easily fall into the habit of feeling that they are better than everyone else. They feel like their possessions entitle them to be treated better than the common people. They forget that **we are all the same in the sight of God**. Many of the rich and the affluent consider themselves a higher class of people both in the world and in the church.

I remember a recent situation reported on the news. A prominent preacher's wife from Houston, Texas, was taking a flight. The flight attendant asked her to do something (which she should have done like everyone else), and her response to the flight attendant was, "Do you know who I am?" What difference did it make who she was or who her husband was? Yet, she felt the **rules did not apply to her because her husband was the pastor of a large church**.

This is the attitude we must be careful about outside and inside of the church, especially if we are rich and affluent. What made this situation so bad was that **she was a pastor's wife**, a person who is **supposed to show forth a Christ-like attitude** to the world. The scriptures teach that this is the attitude God hates. So be careful how you act toward those around you, because **God is keeping a record**.

James 5:2-3

[2] Your riches are corrupted, and your garments are motheaten.
[3] Your gold and silver is cankered; and the rust of them shall be a witness against you, and shall eat your flesh as it were fire. Ye have heaped treasure together for the last days.

In this second verse, James is telling the rich that **their riches were corrupted because of the way that they were**

acquired. What was he saying to the rich, exactly? He was saying that their wealth was gotten by unscrupulous means and that their ill-gotten gain would **not do them any good when it came to the judgement**. All that they possessed would pass to others; and then what would their fate be? By saying that their garments were motheaten, James was saying that their **lifestyles were corrupt**. They lived unsatisfying lives mostly full of sin and shame, and all they were doing would come to nothing.

As I have already said, being rich is not a sin. The Law of Moses gives rules **for the gaining of wealth**. We read of the law referencing **provisions for the Jewish people** in the book of Luke.

Luke 12:16-19

> *16 And he spake a parable unto them, saying, The ground of a certain rich man brought forth plentifully:*
> *17 And he thought within himself, saying, What shall I do, because I have no room where to bestow my fruits?*
> *18 And he said, This will I do: I will pull down my barns, and build greater; and there will I bestow all my fruits and my goods.*
> *19 And I will say to my soul, Soul, thou hast much goods laid up for many years; take thine ease, eat, drink, and be merry.*

As verse three continues, we find that gold and silver will canker away. James brings out that the lust for riches is like a fire that burns within us to the point that man is consumed by his desires. We should understand that money is not sinful; money is only something to be **used for good or bad**. It is the love of money that is the root of all evil.

1 Timothy 6:10-11

> *[10] For the love of money is the root of all evil: which while some coveted after, they have erred from the faith, and pierced themselves through with many sorrows.*
> *[11] But thou, O man of God, flee these things; and follow after righteousness, godliness, faith, love, patience, meekness.*

The love of money causes man to do some very evil things: stealing, killing, lying, adultery and envy; these are all the results of a love of money. The rich can heap together riches; however, on the day of God's judgement, their riches will profit them nothing when they stand before a just God. It will make no difference what your name is or what you have, not even what you have done.

James 5:4

> *Behold, the hire of the labourers who have reaped down your fields, which is of you kept back by fraud, crieth: and the cries of them which have reaped are entered into the ears of the Lord of sabaoth.*

James now begins to talk about a practice that was taking place in Israel. The rich and wealthy landowners were cheating their hired workers out of their just wages. This was strictly forbidden by the Law of Moses. When God gave the law, He **made provisions for the hired laborers and their protection**

201

from those who would misuse them. In Deuteronomy, God's Word says that before the sun went down, the workers were to be paid the wage they had agreed on.

Deuteronomy 24:14-15

> *14 Thou shalt not oppress an hired servant that is poor and needy, whether he be of thy brethren, or of thy strangers that are in thy land within thy gates:*
> *15 At his day thou shalt give him his hire, neither shall the sun go down upon it; for he is poor, and setteth his heart upon it: lest he cry against thee unto the LORD, and it be sin unto thee.*

Other scriptures that deal with the poor and their treatment are found in Proverbs. God in His wisdom **knew the future and made the poor and needy one of His prime concerns**.

Proverbs 14:31

> *He that oppresseth the poor reproacheth his Maker: but he that honoureth him hath mercy on the poor.*

Proverbs 22:16

> *He that oppresseth the poor to increase his riches, and he that giveth to the rich, shall surely come to want.*

James speaks of the rich holding back the pay of the poor and needy. This was wrong according to the Ten Commandments, as well as the Law of Moses. The relevant commandment teaches us: **Thou shalt not steal.**

Now, my Christian brothers and sisters, let us look at one more important lesson from God's Word. It is vital that we, as Christians, pay our bills. When we do **not pay that which we owe according to God's Word**, we are a thief. Remember the **eyes of the Lord are over the righteous**, and God most certainly keeps a record of those who oppress the poor and needy.

James 5:5-6

⁵ Ye have lived in pleasure on the earth, and been wanton; ye have nourished your hearts, as in a day of slaughter.
⁶ Ye have condemned and killed the just; and he doth not resist you.

James continues his thoughts on the rich of his day, how they have abused the poor and needy. James talks about how the rich have lived in pleasure. How their desires have never been satisfied, that they continually want more. Their thoughts are always on ways to fulfill their wanton desires. When the flesh and not the spirit of God leads men and women, they are capable of doing anything and everything. The flesh knows no boundaries. It has no compassion for anyone. Jesus gives us the story of a certain rich man who could have had compassion on a beggar named Lazarus. However, he chose not to and suffered because of it. The rich man wanted everything and did not want the poor man to have anything.

Luke 16:19-31

¹⁹ There was a certain rich man, which was clothed in

purple and fine linen, and fared sumptuously every day:

²⁰ *And there was a certain beggar named Lazarus, which was laid at his gate, full of sores,*

²¹ *And desiring to be fed with the crumbs which fell from the rich man's table: moreover the dogs came and licked his sores.*

²² *And it came to pass, that the beggar died, and was carried by the angels into Abraham's bosom: the rich man also died, and was buried;*

²³ *And in hell he lift up his eyes, being in torments, and seeth Abraham afar off, and Lazarus in his bosom.*

²⁴ *And he cried and said, Father Abraham, have mercy on me, and send Lazarus, that he may dip the tip of his finger in water, and cool my tongue; for I am tormented in this flame*

²⁵ *But Abraham said, Son, remember that thou in thy lifetime receivedst thy good things, and likewise Lazarus evil things: but now he is comforted, and thou art tormented.*

²⁶ *And beside all this, between us and you there is a great gulf fixed: so that they which would pass from hence to you cannot; neither can they pass to us, that would come from thence.*

²⁷ *Then he said, I pray thee therefore, father, that thou wouldest send him to my father's house:*

²⁸ *For I have five brethren; that he may testify unto them, lest they also come into this place of torment.*

²⁹ *Abraham saith unto him, They have Moses and the prophets; let them hear them.*

³⁰ *And he said, Nay, father Abraham: but if one went unto them from the dead, they will repent.*

³¹ And he said unto him, If they hear not Moses and the prophets, neither will they be persuaded, though one rose from the dead.

As we read the scriptures, we can see Lazarus **begging for food as the rich man rides by,** upset because Lazarus did not move from his gate. As the Word says, pride goes before a fall, and the rich man was soon to take the greatest fall of his life. We never know the day nor the hour when we will leave this world. Therefore, it behooves us to **walk upright before the Lord at all times.** We must be careful **not to abuse the poor and the needy.**

At this point, I must **in all good conscience as a man of God** warn my brothers and sisters in Christ to **be wise concerning unscrupulous preachers.** You can see them on TV and hear them on the radio every day. They come begging for money, using gimmicks and trickery. I am not telling you that you should not give money. I am saying to **seek God about it first,** and then if God approves it, **obey the Lord and give.**

Know the ministry you support. I had a fellow pastor who supported a certain "so called" missionary that had an orphanage in Haiti. They supported his orphanage every month until it came out that he had no orphanage in Haiti. This missionary would go to Haiti about once a year. There he would visit an orphanage, take a lot of pictures, return to the States, and put the pictures in his mail outs, while telling the people that it was his orphanage.

He was a liar and a thief; he made merchandise of God's people. **Know those whom you support, who you give your money to.** God expects us to be **wise in our service** toward Him. Know those who labor among you.

As James states in verse six, where he talks about the rich and those who are striving to be rich, *"Ye have condemned and killed the just.*" God is not blind, and I am sure that as the scripture states, He is keeping a record. One day we will face our judgement day. What will your record say about you?

James 5:7-8

⁷ Be patient therefore, brethren, unto the coming of the Lord. Behold, the husbandman waiteth for the precious fruit of the earth, and hath long patience for it, until he receive the early and latter rain.
⁸ Be ye also patient; stablish your hearts: for the coming of the Lord draweth nigh.

James brings up the subject of patience. We find all through the scriptures that God wants us, as believers, to learn patience. Patience is **learning to wait for a certain outcome**. In the natural, we must learn to wait for certain things to take place. An example is waiting to find the perfect mate. When we get in too much of a hurry, we sometimes make mistakes. Thus, patience is **being willing to wait**. In verse seven, James uses the example of being a **farmer to show what he is telling us**.

The farmer is one person who must learn patience. Once he plants the seed, **nothing he does can make it grow or mature any faster**. He must wait for the seed to sprout and come up, then he can only watch it grow, praying that God will, when needed, send the rain. Slowly, the grain **begins to mature, and still he must wait** until the grain has dried enough to reap. Then and only then can the reaper enter the field to bring in the harvest. Make no mistake, the farmer does not sit idly waiting for the grain. He must be **doing his everyday duties along with preparing for the coming harvest**. We do all that we can do, **trusting God to send**

the former and the latter rain along with the sunshine to produce the increase, the harvest.

As the farmer in the natural must wait, **so must we learn to wait before God.** We must prepare for a life of service to God while **waiting for our precious Lord Jesus** to return. The only part that is hard is when we pray and ask God to teach us patience. Why, you ask? **The learning of patience only comes through trials and tribulations.** I know that we grumble about going through trials, however, every trial brings us closer to God and makes us stronger spiritually. When trials and tribulations come, **give God thanks, because He is drawing us closer together** with Him. Meanwhile, keep in mind that the Lord will **never put more upon us than we are able to bear.** Yes, we all have said, "I just wish that He did not think that I could bear so much." Child of God, He loves you and **will always do what is best for you.** As the scripture states, we must establish our hearts in God and the things of God. We must become **rooted and grounded in the words of the gospel** if we are to overcome the storms of this life.

Isaiah 26:3

> *Thou wilt keep him in perfect peace, whose mind is stayed on thee: because he trusteth in thee.*

Brothers and sisters in Christ, know that the devil hates you and his desire for you is to bring you down to an eternal hell where there is weeping and gnashing of teeth.

Matthew 25:30

> *And cast ye the unprofitable servant into outer darkness:*

there shall be weeping and gnashing of teeth.

God loves you and His desire is to bring you **into His kingdom and into His house,** a place we call Heaven. The question for mankind to decide is where they want to spend eternity.

James is very concerned about **the souls of people and concerned about where they will spend** eternity. Yet here he is **writing to the church because of how they are living.** He is troubled about the confusion and turmoil that is happening in local churches. He is trying to teach the saints that **they need to be patient and let the Lord work out their problems.** We must learn that victory comes to those who endure.

The Wiersbe Bible Commentary: NT tells us:

> Here, then, is a secret of endurance when the going is tough: *God is producing a harvest in our lives.* He wants the "fruit of the Spirit" to grow (Gal. 5:22-23), and the only way He can do it is through trials and troubles. Instead of growing impatient with God and with ourselves, we must yield to the Lord and permit the fruit to grow. We are "spiritual farmers" looking for a harvest.
>
> You can enjoy this kind of a harvest only if your heart is *established* (James 5:8). One of the purposes of the spiritual ministry of the local church is to establish the heart (Rom. 1:11). Paul sent Timothy to Thessalonica to establish the young Christians in their faith (1 Thess. 3:1-3), and Paul also prayed for them that they might be established

(1 Thess. 3:10-13). The ministry of the Word of God and prayer are important if the heart is going to be established. A heart that is not established cannot bear fruit.

James' greatest hope in the Lord was that the **saints would become the true servants** that God would have them to be. To have true peace in our hearts, we must be **committed to our Lord**, Jesus Christ, and **totally submitted to Him**. Total submission to God is our only hope for the future and **an eternity in the kingdom of Heaven**. Jesus is coming back very, very soon.

James 5:9

Grudge not one against another, brethren, lest ye be condemned: behold, the judge standeth before the door.

James begins this verse with a warning that we are to **be in control of ourselves**. We are to be careful of our attitude towards others. We are **not to bear hard feelings** toward others for what they do. He is warning us that if we begrudge one another, we will be condemned of God. God tells us that we are **not to judge one another for He is the Judge**. When we place judgement on those around us, then we are in the wrong as much as they are. Remember, God stands at the door and **God does the judging, not us**.

James 5:10

Take, my brethren, the prophets, who have spoken in the name of the Lord, for an example of suffering affliction, and of patience.

In this verse, James gives us an example of suffering. He states that if you want to know about suffering, **look at the lives of the prophets**. We often grumble and complain about the things we are going through. However, child of God, as long as we live for God, we will face trials and troubles. James tells us to look at the prophets. They faced persecutions just as we do and worse. Paul wrote in II Timothy 3:12 that **if we will live for God, we are going to face persecution**. *"Yea, and all that will live godly in Christ Jesus shall suffer persecution."* We are no better than those who have gone before, and we will **surely face the same persecution**.

God called out the prophets in times of conflict and crisis. Their calling was not to **be everyone's friend or to influence the populace**. They were called to **preach the truth whether the people liked it or not**, and they often did not like what they were told. The prophets had to be **men of courage submitted unto the Lord**. Their lives were not glamorous, and most of the time they were shunned by the people. Their persecutions and sufferings were not only at the hands of the unbelievers; sadly, it was also at the hands of those who professed to be followers of God.

The John Phillips Commentary Series reveals:

> For the most part, the prophets were highly unpopular preachers to the consciences of their countrymen. Hosea was a man of sorrows and acquainted with grief. Amos was doubtless popular enough in Israel—as long as he denounced the surrounding nations—but the high priest of the calf

cult threatened him at once when he denounced Israel. Micah was the first prophet to threaten Jerusalem with destruction. He must have been about as popular as a skunk at a Sunday school picnic! Habakkuk was called upon to utter woe after woe against his countrymen. Haggai saw success, but his contemporary and colleague Zechariah was murdered. Isaiah, after a distinguished career, was sawn in half in a hollow tree by Manasseh. And as for Jeremiah, he wept his way through life. John the Baptist was murdered, and so was Jesus.

I can tell you for a fact that when you are a preacher of righteousness, the world will not receive you. Yes, today there are some preachers who seem to be superstars, men and women who are self-serving, who promote themselves more than they promote Jesus Christ, our Saviour. However, praise the Lord, **there are a few who still promote Jesus Christ**. Thank God for men and women who are more interested in preaching the truth than garnering personal acclaim. The pulpit is a place to **preach the truth of the gospel**, not to preach the message of self and the world. Rest assured that **if you preach the Word of God, you will be tested and tried**.

James 5:11

Behold, we count them happy which endure. Ye have heard of the patience of Job, and have seen the end of the Lord; that the Lord is very pitiful, and of tender mercy.

James brings to our attention that we should **count it all joy when we fall into divers (or various) temptations**. The trials and temptations that we experience **let us know that we are still walking with the Lord**. If we were not, then the devil would not be tempting us. In the midst of trials, it is hard to **count ourselves as happy**. However, we need to. We need to **set in our mind certain facts**. One is that there can be no victories until we have **won the battles**. There can be no mountaintop experiences until we have **gone through the valleys**. One of the problems we have is that we want God's best without the pain of spiritual growth. Child of God, it is God's will for us to **grow and prosper and to do well**.

When God gives us privileges, He demands that we **conduct ourselves in a Christ-like manner** keeping certain responsibilities before Him. One of those responsibilities is to **read and study God's precious Holy Word**, the Bible. In the scriptures, there is **knowledge and understanding that is vital** in our walk with the Master. In the scriptures, we find **examples for us to use as patterns for our lives**. These examples cover many of the trials that we are destined to go through. James points us to one of the examples, **the patience of Job**.

As we look at the story of Job, we find that Job *"was perfect and upright, and one that feared God, and eschewed evil."* (Job 1:1) Job was a **very rich man in this world's goods**. He had a **large family, a wife, seven sons and three daughters**. The scriptures tell of a day when the sons of God came to **present themselves before the Lord**, and Satan came among them. The Lord asked Satan where he had been, and he told Him, "Walking back and forth in the earth and up and down in it." The Lord then asked Satan if **he had considered his servant Job**. Whereupon, Satan told the Lord that Job had reason to fear the Lord and that

He had a hedge built around Job and all that he possessed. Satan then told God that if God would **remove His hand of protection from Job and his possessions,** things would be different. The Lord told Satan all that Job had was no longer protected, except that **Satan could not touch Job's life**.

Satan began his work on Job. He was determined to **prove to God that he could and would break Job**. Before long, one of Job's servants came running to tell Job that the Sabeans had stolen all his oxen and donkeys then killed his servants. While this servant was talking, another came running in. The second servant proceeded to report that a fire fell from heaven and burned up or killed all his sheep and the servants that kept watch over them, and he was the only one to survive.

While this was still taking place, yet another servant came running in to report that the Chaldeans had stolen all his camels and killed his servants. All this Satan did on the same day; however, Satan was not finished yet. One more servant came running in to tell Job that all ten of his children and their servants were dead, all in one day.

Job, I am sure, was devastated. The scriptures say that Job **got up, rent his clothes, shaved his head**, fell upon the ground and **began to worship God**. This is when Job uttered those never-forgotten words; *"Naked came I out of my mother's womb, and naked shall I return thither: the Lord gave, and the Lord hath taken away: blessed be the name of the Lord. In all of this Job sinned not, nor charged God foolishly."* (Job 1:20-22) I am sure Satan was pleased because of what he had done to Job.

Again, there came a day when the **sons of God came to present themselves before the Lord,** and Satan came along with them to present himself to the Lord. Again, the Lord asked Satan where he had been. Satan told God that he had been **going**

throughout the world. The Lord again asked Satan, "Have you considered my servant Job? There is none like him in the earth. He is a perfect and upright man, one who fears God." The Lord told Satan that **even after all he had done to Job, he had kept his integrity and had not sinned**.

Satan told the Lord, "*Skin for skin, yea, all that a man hath will he give for his life.*" (Job 2:4) Satan said that if God would "put forth your hand now, and touch his bone and his flesh," He would see Job curse Him to His face. Then the Lord told Satan he could do what he desired, however **he could not touch Job's life**, because it **belonged to God**. Therefore, Satan went forth and smote Job with sores and boils from the soles of his feet to the crown of his head. Job went out and sat in the ash pile and scraped the boils. As this was happening, Job's wife told him, "Are you going to continue serving God? Why do you not just go ahead, curse God and die?" **Job replied and said, "You talk like a foolish woman."**

To complicate things, Job's **three friends came by to see him**. For seven days and nights they sat upon the ground with Job and said nothing, for Job was in very great grief. Then Job began to speak, saying that he cursed the day of his birth. This does not mean that Job used bad language (cussing); it means that Job regretted the day he was born, that he wished he had never been conceived, or had died at birth. His friends did not help him at all. They believed that his troubles all came upon him because he did something wrong. **Yet, Job's faith in God remained strong.** He knew in whom he believed and that He was **well able to keep that which was committed unto Him**.

The patience of Job, and his **faith and trust in God**, won Job the victory. Job lost his riches and his children. He suffered unbelievable pain at the loss of his children, at his affliction, and because his friends did not believe him. However, Job was **patient in his trust in God**. Job did not understand why all of this was happening to him, he just knew that **God had His reasons and he was not going to turn away from God**. Because of Job's faith, God repaid him by **giving him twice what he had possessed before plus ten more children**.

It is Satan's plan and desire to get us to become impatient with God. Impatience causes us to make bad judgement calls. When we get emotional, we lose calm thought. To win the victory, we must **be patient and submitted to God**.

The Wiersbe Bible Commentary: NT says:

> When you find yourself in the furnace, go to the throne of grace and receive from the Lord all the grace you need to endure (Heb.4:14-16). Remind yourself that the Lord has a gracious purpose in all of this suffering, and that He will work out His purposes in His time and for His glory. You are not a robot caught in the jaws of fate. You are a loving child of God, privileged to be a part of a wonderful plan. There is a difference!

Trials and temptations come to Christians for many reasons. One is to **teach patience and trust in God**. Another is that suffering builds character, and **character is what we need to establish a Christian life**, a life of trust, patience, and submission. In this life, we are waiting for our Lord, Jesus Christ, to return. We must be **patient and vigilant looking for His return**. Remember that **Jesus is merciful to His children**.

James 5:12

But above all things, my brethren, swear not, neither by heaven, neither by the earth, neither by any other oath: but let your yea be yea; and your nay, nay; lest ye fall into condemnation.

James now tells us to be **very careful in what we swear to**. He states that it is better **not to swear at all**. Have you ever asked yourself why it is that we feel the need to swear an oath? Scripture tells us to let our yea be yea, and our nay be nay (or yes be yes and no be no). Yet, there seems to be that overwhelming need to swear that we are telling the truth. It is as if we do not believe a person can tell the truth unless they swear or give an oath to speak true. The Christian should **always speak the truth without the need to swear an oath**. God's Word instructs us to always speak the truth; lying should not even be an option for a Christian. If we claim to be a Christian and tell lies, then our witness is in vain and our life is vain. A liar is not (nor can be) a Christian until they **repent and ask for forgiveness** before Christ. Always be truthful, and you will never be caught in a lie.

James 5:13-15

[13] Is any among you afflicted? let him pray. Is any merry? let him sing psalms.
[14] Is any sick among you? let him call for the elders of the church; and let them pray over him, anointing him with oil in the name of the Lord:
[15] And the prayer of faith shall save the sick, and the Lord

shall raise him up; and if he have committed sins, they
shall be forgiven him.

I have grouped these scriptures together since they all deal with each other. James begins verse thirteen with: "*Is any among you afflicted? Let him pray.*" James did not ask about those sick or diseased. He used **the word afflicted**, which can relate **to any kind of hardship** a person might be facing. His answer to them was to pray, to **take it to the Lord**. In serving God, the Lord does not leave us to our own resources. He is a **constant help in the time of trouble**. He will never leave us nor forsake us. "*Let your conversation be without covetousness; and be content with such things as ye have: for he hath said, I will never leave thee, nor forsake thee.*" (Hebrews 13:5)

There is an old song by H. F. Lyte and Wm. H. Monk called *Abide With Me*. Part of it goes like this:

> Abide with me! Fast falls the even-tide,
> The darkness deepens – Lord, with me abide!
> When other helpers fail, and comforts flee,
> Help of the helpless, oh, abide with me!
>
> Hold Thou Thy cross before my closing eyes;
> Shine thru' the gloom, and point me to the skies;
> Heav'n's morning breaks and earth's vain shadows
>   flee!
> In life, in death, O Lord, abide with me!

The last part of James 5:13 tells us that if we are happy, we should **show it to the world**. A good way to reveal this happiness is to sing or hum to yourself. You can even **sing aloud**

217

so that others can hear your song of happiness and rejoice with you.

In the fourteenth verse we read: *"Is any sick among you? let him call for the elders of the church; and let them pray over him, anointing him with oil in the name of the Lord:"* This is one way God has **laid out for the sick to be healed**. Prayer works today just as it did when James laid out this pattern for us to follow. **Prayer is God's method for healing**, and God moves when people pray. The only limits that God has are the limits that we place on Him by our unbelief. Healing is the children's bread; all we need to do is to **get out of the way and let God do what needs doing**.

There are those today who do not believe that God will heal or work miracles in our time, as He did for the apostles and others in the early churches. Sadly for them, God will not – not because He does not want to, but because **their unbelief stands in the way**. They need to know that what Peter spoke in Acts 10:34 is still true today: *"that God is no respecter of persons:"* We are healed by the stripes that were laid upon Jesus' back. Healing is ours; **the thirty-nine stripes laid upon our Lord purchased our healing**. Even the prophet Isaiah prophesied of future healing.

Isaiah 53:4-5

> [4] *Surely he hath borne our griefs, and carried our sorrows: yet we did esteem him stricken, smitten of God, and afflicted.*
> [5] *But he was wounded for our transgressions, he was bruised for our iniquities: the chastisement of our peace was upon him; and with his stripes we are healed.*

Also, in 1 Peter 2:24, we find where Peter is telling us that **by the stripes that were laid upon Jesus' back**, we were healed. Note the difference between Isaiah and I Peter. Isaiah states that by His stripes **we *are* healed**; while Peter tells us that by His stripes **we *were* healed**. What Peter is saying is that we are already healed; all we have to do is **use our faith**, go before God according to scripture and believe. Again, in Mark, we find where the Word tells us to **lay hands upon the sick and pray the prayer of faith** and they shall recover.

A Bible Study on the Holy Ghost by David D. Wilson states:

> Laying hands on the sick, by believers, and anointing with oil by the elders are two ways through which the gifts of healings operate. Healing is the mending of the body when it is sick or diseased. There is also a spiritual healing that takes place when we are spiritually hurt. We call the blind receiving their sight a miracle, but it isn't; it's a healing. Deaf ears unstopped, crooked limbs made straight and cancers disappearing, all this is healing.
>
> One of the greatest modern day preachers who had the gift of healing was Smith Wigglesworth. He tries to teach us in his writings that **to pray the prayer of faith for healing or anything else, we first must get our eyes off the sickness and get our eyes on Jesus.** When our eyes are on Jesus, then we can pray effectively, and God answers our prayer. This is faith in action, and the outcome is to

see the hand of God heal or work miracles. But we must keep our eyes upon Jesus.

I feel sorry for people who do not believe that God can heal. They believe that God does not want to heal. Why would they think that a loving and compassionate Father God would not want His children healed? Our Heavenly Father **loves us and cares for us**. It is He whom earthly fathers should pattern themselves after. Why would we believe that God does not heal or work miracles for us today? The God that we serve who **knows when a sparrow falls**, who tells us that He even **knows the numbers of the hairs** that are upon our heads; this God who **promises to go with us to the very end** of our lives, and when we have drawn our last breath, **usher us into His glorious kingdom** to live with Him forever where all is love and peace and there will never be any more sickness, heartache or pain, **why would He not heal** our bodies?

Many denominations believe the days of great healing and miracles are past. They teach that the gifts of healing, miracles and tongues such as the gifts of the apostles were temporary and were used for a period of transition in the early church. They teach that the Jews rejected the spirit of God, causing God to withdraw the signs and gifts, and they are not for us today. One writer wrote that when people are healed in healing services, it is in spite of so-called healers. It is God answering the prayers of the people. Do they not know that **any healing is God answering the prayer** of His people? My word of encouragement to you is to never take man's word for anything. **Believe what the Bible says.** It states that **God heals and works miracles because He loves us and He cares about us**.

Verse fifteen tells us what will happen when we are

obedient to the Word. The prayer of faith shall **save the sick and the Lord shall raise them up** just as the Word says. Healing is **ours through the blood** of Jesus. There are many Christians in many denominations who are suffering from sicknesses of all kinds, not trusting and believing that Jesus can heal. They have been told that God no longer heals and works miracles, so they suffer. Their only hope is in what man can do. How pitiful the church has become with so little faith in God! Whatever happened to **trusting and obeying what the Word** says? In 1 John 5:14-15, it teaches us that if we have confidence in God, God will move in our behalf.

There are those in the ministry who teach that all sickness is the result of some sin that you have committed. This is one of the most ridiculous things I have ever heard. I will agree that some sickness is the result of sin, just not all sickness. An example is some forms of cancer are the result of sin, just not all cancer. Venereal disease is a result of sin by someone, if not you, maybe by your mate or parents. However, with AIDS, people have gotten it through blood transfusions or blood contact or even from being bitten by a person with AIDS. Not all sickness is a result of sin. People who think so are showing their ignorance. It is not Biblical. This is why the scripture states that *if* they have sinned, their sin will be forgiven them. Praise God for forgiveness.

James 5:16

Confess your faults one to another, and pray one for another, that ye may be healed. The effectual fervent prayer of a righteous man availeth much.

221

In this verse, James tells the people to **confess their faults one to another**. It is important that we **pray one for another**, and that we **stand before God for our brothers and sisters** in Christ. I would say this, when it comes to confessing our faults to each other, be careful. **Know those around you.** Know those in whom you put your trust. Not all people are what they appear to be. Just because they claim to be a good Christian does not mean they are. Gossip has ruined more friendships and torn up more churches than anything I know. Therefore, my brothers and sisters, **be very careful whom you confess to or confide in**.

Once you know whom you can trust and whom you cannot, then and only then **tell your fellow Christian friends the things you need prayed over**, knowing that the scripture tells us that the **effectual fervent prayer of a righteous man avails much**. As we study the scriptures, we find that the **prayers of the saints are never in vain**. In Revelation, we read that the **prayers of the saints are kept in vials** before God.

Revelation 5:8

> *And when he had taken the book, the four beasts and four and twenty elders fell down before the Lamb, having every one of them harps, and golden vials full of odours, which are the prayers of saints.*

Revelation 8:3-4

> *[3] And another angel came and stood at the altar, having a golden censer; and there was given unto him much incense, that he should offer it with the prayers of all saints upon the golden altar which was before the throne.*

⁴ And the smoke of the incense, which came with the prayers of the saints, ascended up before God out of the angel's hand.

Here in Revelation 8:3 we learn that the prayers of the saints are **offered up before God upon the golden altar by the angels**. Therefore, the **prayers of the saints ascend before God**; this is why we know that God takes notice of our prayers. God **hears and answers our prayers in spite of all the devil can do and others say**.

Now you ask, if God answers prayer, then why do people get sick and stay sick when people are praying for them? We must remember that **what God does and allows is for a reason**. An example: A man who had a brother who was **saved when he was seven years old**. Then somewhere in his childhood, he walked away from his salvation and God. His mother prayed and prayed for him. It seemed that everyone's prayers did no good. Then his mother became very ill and died. Her death affected him so greatly that he **started going back to church**. He prayed through and **recommitted his life to God**; he stayed committed until he died. He made the statement that **his mother's death was what brought him back to God**. Never think that God does not care. He does, and He knows what it will take to get your prayers answered. **Only believe, my friend**. Only believe that your prayers never go in vain.

James 5:17-18

¹⁷ Elias was a man subject to like passions as we are, and he prayed earnestly that it might not rain: and it rained not on the earth by the space of three years and six

223

months.

[18] And he prayed again, and the heaven gave rain, and the earth brought forth her fruit.

James in these two verses gives us **a perfect example of God hearing and answering prayer**. He introduces us to the prophet Elijah, a man called by God and chosen of God to do a work in Israel. King Ahab and Queen Jezebel had led the nation into idolatry and become worshipers of the idol Baal. Therefore, God called a man to stand before the nation proclaiming judgement and to **ask the people to return to God**.

What kind of man was Elijah? Not much is known about Elijah's life before God called him. James speaks of Elijah as being a man **subject to like passions as are we**. We do know that Elijah was **a righteous man**, or he would not have had the Lord's calling. Like all people, Elijah was a man with faults and failures. However, like all the saints, we must **rise above all that would hold us down and serve the Lord** to the best of our abilities.

In obeying the Lord, Elijah prayed, and it rained not on the earth for three and a half years. The Word states that **Elijah prayed earnestly, which means that he was serious with God**, and God honored his prayer. I may have touched on this before, however, there is a great deal of difference between praying a prayer and just saying a prayer. Most people just say a prayer, and such a prayer does very little good. On the other hand, the man or woman who **prays in earnest sincerity, their prayer rises up before God and God answers**.

At the end of the three and a half years, Elijah prayed again, and the heavens gave forth an abundance of rain. The earth **once more gave forth her abundance of fruit and flowers**. The rain stopped because the man of God prayed, and the rains came

224

again when the **man of God prayed asking for rain**. Prayer works when we are **earnest and sincere before God**. So, let us pray for **a great revival once more**.

James 5:19-20

[19] Brethren, if any of you do err from the truth, and one convert him;
[20] Let him know, that he which converteth the sinner from the error of his way shall save a soul from death, and shall hide a multitude of sins.

James closes his epistle with a **burden on his heart for the lost backsliders**. Perhaps James knew some who had once believed the truth and erred from the path of holiness before God. In truth, there are many who are backslidden today. It happens in every church. What is the cause? The best way that I can put it is that a person neglects their prayer life and the reading of God's Word. Then slowly they begin to grow spiritually cold in their soul. Then we see them slowly give over to the desires and lust of the fleshly things until finally they have completely walked away from God. Below is an illustration that I like.

The John Phillips Commentary Series reveals:

A famous violinist was asked how long he practiced every day. He replied that he spent ten to twelve hours a day with his instrument. "What would happen if you slacked off?" he was asked.

"After one day," he said, "I would know it. After two days, the conductor would know it. After

225

three days, the orchestra would know it. After that, everybody would know it."

Thus it is when a person slacks off on their prayer life. They begin to suffer spiritually. They can lie to everyone around them, however, they cannot lie to God or themselves.

In verse twenty, James is telling us that one who **reaches out to the backslider and restores them to the fold has done a good work**. He has helped **save a soul from the pits of hell**, and because of his or her efforts, a **multitude of sins have been forgiven and washed away** forever. Child of God, heaven will be worth **whatever price that we have to pay**. Serve God, live every day for him, be a **witness to this lost and dying world** and help save a soul from sin.

Chapter 5 Review Questions

1. What are the two main parts of this fifth chapter?

_____

_____

2. Is being rich in this world's goods a sin?

_____

3. What was James saying to the rich in verses 2-3?

_____

_____

_____

4. James brings out how that the lust for riches is like a . . .

_____

5. In the Bible. when were workers to receive their pay?

_____

_____

6. Patience only comes through . . .

_____

_____

7. Where does Paul say that we will face persecution?

_____

_____

8. When God gives us privileges, He demands that we conduct ourselves in a . . .

_____

_____

_____

9. How many children did Job have?

_____

_____

10. What does impatience cause a Christian to make?

_____

_____

11. What will you never be caught doing if you always tell the truth?

_____

_____

12. What does the word afflicted mean?

_____

_____

_____

13. In Hebrews 13:5, the Lord tells us that He will never do

something. What is it?

_____

_____

_____

14. What are we to do when sickness comes according to the

scriptures?

_____

_____

_____

15. What are the only limits that God has?

_____

_____

_____

16. How many stripes were laid upon the back of Jesus?

_____

17. What is the difference between what Isaiah wrote in the Old Testament and that written by Peter in the New Testament about the stripes on Jesus' back?

_____

_____

_____

18. Is all sickness the result of us committing sin?

_____

_____

19. Are we to confess our faults to just anyone who claims to be a Christian?

_____

20. What do we read about the prayers of the saints in the book of Revelation?

_____

_____

21. How long did it not rain after Elijah prayed and asked God to stop the rain?

_____

22. Yes or No. Is there a difference between saying a prayer and praying a prayer? What is the difference?

_____

_____

_____

23. What would you say is the first step taken toward backsliding?

_____

_____

_____

24. What does verse twenty tell us about the person who leads a backslider back to God?

_____

_____

_____

Acknowledgment

In our service of the Lord, there are many tools for us to use. We have the Bible, God's Holy Word, and then we have Bible commentaries and studies to help enlighten the scripture to us. I know that we all do not believe exactly alike. Yet there is some good in every commentary. As I was once told about commentaries, it is like eating grapes. You eat the grape and spit out the seeds.

At this time, I would like to say again as I have said at other times that I would like to give wholehearted thanks to the authors and printers of the books and publications listed below. Without their hard work and input, this Bible study could not have been written.

It is not my desire to write a textbook or commentary, but only to write a simple Bible study on God's Word, which can be used by those seeking a deeper understanding of the Holy Scriptures as a group or by an individual. The authors listed below have a deep insight into the Holy Scriptures, and I have quoted much from some of these authors' work.

I can recommend without hesitation their work to you. I believe that the Bible teaches us that we must study to show ourselves approved unto God. Without a clear understanding of God's Word, we fall prey to the tricks of the devil, and we cannot live a consistent Christian life. I hope and pray that this simple Bible study will help you to have a fuller understanding of God's precious Holy Word and answer some of the questions that you may have.

May God bless you and lead you into the truth of His Word. Remember, only believe, for all things are possible if we will only believe. Use what God has given to you to become the man or woman that God desires you to be. Pray and study, and ask God to give you the understanding and wisdom that only He can give. Thank God for His answer and believe.

Bibliography

Rev. Albert Barnes
>   *Barnes' Notes on the New Testament*
>   Baker Book House Company
>   Grand Rapids, Michigan
>   Reprinted 2005
>   Reprinted from the 1847 edition published by Blackie &
>   Son, London

Rev. Warren W. Wiersbe
>   *The Wiersbe Bible Commentary: New Testament*
>   Published by David C. Cook
>   Colorado Springs, Colorado
>   Second Edition 2007

Flavius Josephus (37 AD – 100 AD)
>   *Josephus, The Complete Works of*
>   Translated by William Whiston, A.M.
>   Kregel Publications
>   Grand Rapids, Michigan
>   Copyright 1960

Webster's New World College Dictionary
>   IDG Books Worldwide Inc.
>   An International Data Group Company
>   Foster City, California
>   Fourth Edition
>   Copyright 2000

Rev. John Phillips
The Epistle of James
The John Phillips Commentary Series
Kregel Publications
Grand Rapids, Michigan
Published 2001

Answers
Chapter 1 (Page 78)

1. He was the brother of Jesus
2. James the Lord's brother
3. In the book *The Complete Works of Josephus*
4. He was beaten to death with a club
5. The book of James was written to the members of the twelve tribes, which were scattered abroad.
6. A good follower
7. Mature spiritually
8. They mold and make us into what God desires us to become.
9. That we are willing to stand, regardless of the cost we will stand.
10. We are showing that we are immature, unable to make up our minds.
11. The same problems rise to the surface.
12. A crown of life which the Lord, Himself shall give to us.
13. Trials and test come from God.
14. Temptations come from Satan, for no man is tempted of God.
15. Eve blamed the serpent; Adam blamed Eve and then blamed God because He gave Eve to him.
16. Fault still lies with us and no one else.
17. (a). The devil can try to persuade us to give in to sin, however he cannot force us to sin.

    (b). The devil can put the bait of sin before us; however, he cannot force us to bite the hook of sin.
18. It is his will, with his will he says no to sin or with his will

he says yes to his desires.

19. Salvation through faith
20. Decrease
21. The voice of the Lord
22. Never be unsaid and sometimes it comes back to haunt us.
23. God will give to us the spirit of understanding.
24. Learn how to serve God.
25. What God wants us to be and also it shows us what we truly are like.

Chapter 2 (Page 127)

1. The two main groups of Christians are the fundamentalists and the liberals.
   (a) The fundamentalists believe in the literal truth of God's Word. If the Bible says it then that is how it is.
   (b) The liberals consider themselves to be unbiased and open minded, favoring progressive ideals that do away with the basic truth of the Bible in favor of a very permissive religion.
2. Respect of persons or partiality
3. It has been said that more wars have been fought over religion than any other cause.
4. The most precious thing that a person possess is their everlasting soul.
5. We have been taught from childhood to judge people by their appearance, what we may know about their past life and their financial status.
6. Prejudiced people. By the way they act, they hurt other people's feelings. They cause people to become depressed.
7. God chooses the poor most of the time because they are

238

rich in faith. Because they cannot rely on riches or social status since they have none, they put their faith and trust in God.

8. The beginning of wisdom

9. Carl Marx believed and said, "If you tell a lie long enough it will become the truth." An example is the theory of evolution.

10. The more highly educated people become, the less likely they are to believe in God.

11. The royal law that James speaks of is to "love thy neighbor as thyself."

12. Yes, we must have a Christ-like love for everyone, however we do not have to like their lifestyle or the way that they act.

13. Like so many men today, Solomon's downfall was women.

14. He had seven hundred wives and three hundred concubines.

15. King David committed adultery.

16. No, the sin is when we yield to the temptation.

17. Polytheism is the belief in more than one God.

18. Pantheism is a belief that all of the forces of the universe are God.

19. They, asked Jesus, "Art thou come hither to torment us before the time?"

20. Abraham and Sarah were half brother and sister. Same father – different mothers.

21. Because God honored her faith in risking her life to save and protect the spies.

Chapter 3 (Page 161)

1. The position of being a Rabi or teacher, which was coveted in the early church.
2. It is hard to teach something you know very little about.
3. We are to do what Christ would do. We are to go to them and apologize.
4. The tongue is the most unruly member of the body.
5. Jesus is our spiritual rudder, directing our lives in the right direction.
6. Because they can never be taken back.
7. James tells us, "The tongue can no man tame."
8. Jesus is the only one who can control our tongues.
9. Out of the abundance of the heart, the mouth speaks.
10. In verses eleven and twelve, James uses the spring and how it cannot bring forth sweet water and bitter water at the same time; and how a fig tree cannot produce olives.
11. Wisdom is the ability to use knowledge correctly. Without wisdom, knowledge profits us very little.
12. You cannot fool all of the people all of the time.
13. Pure, peaceable and gentle
14. He walks in the righteousness of Jesus Christ.

Chapter 4 (Page 192)

1. He tells us that wars come from within us.
2. "Ye lust and have not; ye kill and desire to have, and cannot obtain."
3. The world wants no commandments placed upon it.
4. James tells us, "Yye ask, and receive not, because ye ask amiss, that ye may consume it upon your lust."

240

5. Because we have the Bible, God's Word, at our disposal almost everywhere.
6. They are spiritually committing adultery.
7. When we accept Christ as our Saviour, we become a part of the Bride of Christ. Then to commit sin is breaking our vow to God to remain true to Him. Thus, we are committing adultery.
8. People want God to be instant in giving them what they want. They do not want to wait on anything.
9. "Submit yourselves therefore, to God. Resist the devil, and he will flee from you."
10. The spirit of darkness.
11. When we clean up the inner man, the outer man changes to reflect the inner man.
12. When sinners are brought to the realization that they are lost, then God can bring conviction to their hearts.
13. **Psalm 51:16-17 -** *[16] For thou desirest not sacrifice; else would I give it: thou delightest not in burnt offering.*
[17] The sacrifices of God are a broken spirit: a broken and a contrite heart, O God, thou wilt not despise.
14. The Bible, God's Holy Word, was written to the churches and to the saints. It was not written to the sinful world. It was an attempt to keep the church, the saints, prayed up and close to God.
15. Put ourselves into the hands of a merciful God.

Chapter 5 (Page 227)

1. The two main parts of James chapter five is people having trouble and prayer.
2. No

3. He was saying that their wealth was gotten by unscrupulous means and would do them no good in the judgement.
4. A fire that burns within us, to the point that man is consumed by his desire.
5. Workers were to be paid their agreed amount of wages each day before the sun went down.
6. Trials and tribulations
7. II Timothy 3:12
8. Christ-like manner keeping certain responsibilities before Him.
9. Ten children: seven sons and three daughters
10. Bad judgements
11. Lie
12. Any kind of hardship that a person might be facing
13. Leave us nor forsake us
14. Call for the elders of the church to pray over us, anointing us with oil.
15. The ones placed upon him by our unbelief.
16. Thirty-nine stripes, forty save one
17. Isaiah states that by His stripes we **are** healed; while Peter tells us that by his stripes we **were** healed.
18. No, it is not.
19. No, we are to know them who labor among us, we are to know their lives and their relationship with God before we trust them with our troubles.
20. We read in Revelation that the prayers of the saints are bottled up in vials and then offered up on the golden altar before God.
21. Three and a half years
22. Yes. One comes from the mouth and the other from the

heart.

23. Neglecting our prayer life
24. They have saved one from hell and hidden a multitude of sins.

Coming Soon!

A Study on Titus & Philemon

Chapter 1

Titus 1:1-4

¹ Paul, a servant of God, and an apostle of Jesus Christ, according to the faith of God's elect, and the acknowledging of the truth which is after godliness;
² In hope of eternal life, which God, that cannot lie, promised before the world began;
³ But hath in due times manifested his word through preaching, which is committed unto me according to the commandment of God our Saviour;
⁴ To Titus, mine own son after the common faith: Grace, mercy, and peace, from God the Father and the Lord Jesus Christ our Saviour.

In this first verse, Paul declares who he is, **an apostle of Jesus Christ called of God to proclaim the gospel of salvation before a lost and dying world**. Paul, as we know, was a man of faith, a true believer. He was what we all strive to be, **one of God's chosen elect**. He acknowledges the power and the truth that is in Jesus Christ, our Lord. He acknowledges that Jesus is our **one and only Saviour and Redeemer**; that Jesus is the **only redeemer for all of mankind**.

Paul believed in living a life of **holiness and godliness before this present world**. As we give ourselves to Jesus, He

245

begins to change us from the inside out. He teaches us by example that we can **stand upon the promises in God's Holy Word**, for as the scriptures teach, God cannot lie. God established His Precious Holy Word **before the beginning of this world**.

2 Corinthians 7:1

> *Having therefore these promises, dearly beloved, let us cleanse ourselves from all filthiness of the flesh and spirit, perfecting holiness in the fear of God.*

2 Peter 1:3-4

> *3 According as his divine power hath given unto us all things that pertain unto life and godliness, through the knowledge of him that hath called us to glory and virtue:*
> *4 Whereby are given unto us exceeding great and precious promises: that by these ye might be partakers of the divine nature, having escaped the corruption that is in the world through lust.*

The promises of God are eternal; they are **for His children**, the saints. Like Paul, we can **live by them and stand upon them**, because God will **never fail those who live for Him** and serve Him.

As we look at verse three, Paul states that God *"in due times"* has manifested Himself **through the preaching of His Holy Word**. This commission, given to Paul on the Damascus road; was to preach the unsearchable riches of God's glory, so that the **lost souls of this world** might be saved.

1 Corinthians 1:21

For after that in the wisdom of God the world by wisdom knew not God, it pleased God by the foolishness of preaching to save them that believe.

The preaching of the gospel is a **very special calling put upon certain individuals** by God. Paul was such a person along with the other apostles. In God's plan, He has chosen **certain individuals, men and women**, to fill special positions in the work of reaching the lost. Some He calls to be ministers, some to be teachers and some to be missionaries. Whatever the calling may be, God will give **grace and power for you to see your calling through**.

God has a **plan for our lives**. He has **seasons or times when we are to step up and do what God wants done**. Our time may not be God's time; however, **always wait upon God's time**. Never get ahead of God; if you do then you are out there by yourself. Likewise, neither let us lag behind God, for we must **move with God to be profitable**. For to everything there is a season and a time. In Ecclesiastes, we read the writings of Solomon.

Ecclesiastes 3:1-8

¹ To every thing there is a season, and a time to every purpose under the heaven:
² A time to be born, and a time to die; a time to plant, and a time to pluck up that which is planted;
³ A time to kill, and a time to heal; a time to break down,

and a time to build up;

⁴ A time to weep, and a time to laugh; a time to mourn, and a time to dance;

⁵ A time to cast away stones, and a time to gather stones together; a time to embrace, and a time to refrain from embracing;

⁶ A time to get, and a time to lose; a time to keep, and a time to cast away;

⁷ A time to rend, and a time to sew; a time to keep silence, and a time to speak;

⁸ A time to love, and a time to hate; a time of war, and a time of peace.

Just as it states in verse one, *"To every thing there is a season, and a time to every purpose under the heaven."* God has a **plan for our lives if we will live for Him**. That plan is to spread God's Word to the lost or sinners of this sinful world, whether through **preaching or witnessing to those who live around us**.

In verse four, Paul speaks of Titus as being his own son after the common faith. Was Titus Paul's son? Not in the natural; however, he was in the spiritual because **it was Paul who led Titus to Jesus Christ**. Paul's use of "after the common" means that we all are **saved or brought into the same faith by our belief in Jesus Christ** as our personal Saviour and Lord. This is the faith that all born-again believers have in common, a faith common to each other. This faith has **no denominational labels**; it is the same for everyone **if you have been saved**. Born again. We all have this faith in common. It matters not what denomination you belong to, Baptist, Methodist, Church of Christ, Pentecostal or whatever you may be. We all must be **born again**

to enter into the common faith.

Titus 1:5-9

> *⁵ For this cause left I thee in Crete, that thou shouldest set in order the things that are wanting, and ordain elders in every city, as I had appointed thee:*
> *⁶ If any be blameless, the husband of one wife, having faithful children not accused of riot or unruly.*
> *⁷ For a bishop must be blameless, as the steward of God; not selfwilled, not soon angry, not given to wine, no striker, not given to filthy lucre;*
> *⁸ But a lover of hospitality, a lover of good men, sober, just, holy, temperate;*
> *⁹ Holding fast the faithful word as he hath been taught, that he may be able by sound doctrine both to exhort and to convince the gainsayers.*

Paul tells Titus in verse five why he left him in Crete. As we read, we are given to understand that there were problems in the local churches or assemblies. Paul appointed Titus to **act as he would act if he had stayed in Crete**. With this authority, Titus was to **set in order the things that they were wanting or missing**. These churches had not officially been set in a good working order. Some were not much more than prayer meetings with no official head or leaders.

Every assembly **must have a form of leadership that is scripturally sound** in doctrine. Not too much is known about how the services were run: Did they have a Sunday school? I think not. However, I cannot be sure. In the early churches, the emphasis was upon **teaching the gospel message to everyone**

249

who would listen. Yet, the church must be more than a social gathering. Therefore, Titus was left to attend to the work of **setting each congregation in order**. There must be rules of conduct and rules of order for the church to follow. Along with this, there must be **elders ordained in every church**. The elders were men that were given the responsibility of **overseeing the church and its functions**.

Titus had to get to know these men so that he would know their reputations, their manners and how they ran their households; to be sure that they were **worthy of the office to be put upon them**. God is very particular who holds **offices in His church**.

With verse seven, we begin to see the rules Titus was to go by. First, the elders must have **a blameless reputation**. In other words, there could be no accusations of bad conduct leveled against them. Second, they must be the **husband of one wife**. Contrary to what many believe, this does not mean that a divorced man could not have the office of an elder. We need to use some common sense here. In the time of the early church, it was **common for many men to have more than one wife**.

Even in the Jewish law, if a man married, and something happened to him so that he and his wife were childless at the time of his death; then **one of his brothers was to take his widow to be his wife**, and the **first child born to this union was to inherit the dead brother's estate**. Thus, plural marriages were common, among the Jewish people as well as the Gentiles. Just as today, there are places where plural marriages are lawful and widely accepted.

The scripture is merely saying that **to hold the office of an elder, that a man could only have one wife**. Think about it, if a man had more than one wife and had children by them and he came to the Lord and was saved, would it be right for him to divorce all his wives, and their children, except for one wife and her children? It would not be right for him to do this.

You will not find in the scriptures any place where God **specifically states that a man cannot have more** than one wife. In most of this world's countries, plural marriages are illegal, however, not in all of them. There are fifty-eight countries where plural marriages are legal out of the two hundred countries worldwide at the time this book was written.

Therefore, the scripture means just what it says. To be an elder, **a man can only be married to one woman at a time** . . .

You will want your own copy of this exciting new study coming soon at www.ParadiseGospelPress.com.

www.ingramcontent.com/pod-product-compliance
Lightning Source LLC
Chambersburg PA
CBHW060305100426
42742CB00011B/1877